AMERICA'S BLESSINGS

America's Blessings

How Religion Benefits Everyone,
Including Atheists

R ODNEY S TARK

✳ ✳ ✳

TEMPLETON PRESS

Templeton Press
300 Conshohocken State Road, Suite 500
West Conshohocken, PA 19428
www.templetonpress.org

Designed and typeset by Gopa & Ted2, Inc.

Library of Congress Cataloging-in-Publication Data

Stark, Rodney.
America's blessings : how religion benefits everyone, including
atheists / Rodney Stark.
    p. cm.
Includes bibliographical references and index.
ISBN 978-1-59947-412-0 (hardback : alk. paper) 1. Christianity—
United States. 2. Christianity—Influence. 3. Christianity and
culture—United States. I. Title.
BR517.S725 2012
200.973—dc23
                                                    2012016177

Printed in the United States of America

12 13 14 15 16 17   10 9 8 7 6 5 4 3 2 1

Contents

AMERICA'S BLESSINGS

Introduction

I N 1630 the Pilgrim leader John Winthrop described his
vision for a new North American society as "a shining city
upon a hill," a special nation blessed by God. Since then, this
image of America has often been repeated by prominent Americans, especially by presidents, who have regarded it as intrinsic
to American exceptionalism. It is an image that many liberals find embarrassing and many conservatives regard as self-
evident—but nearly everyone admits one of its fundamental
assumptions: America is an unusually religious nation. Nearly
all Americans say they believe in God, about 80 percent believe
in heaven, about 70 percent believe in hell, and half pray at least
once a day (32 percent pray more than once).[1]

Many American "intellectuals," especially those who frequent faculty lounges and staff the national news media, regret
these facts of our religious life. In doing so, they overlook a
remarkable truth: Americans benefit immensely from being an
unusually religious people—blessings that not only fall upon
believers but also on those Americans who most oppose religion. In America, militant atheists are far less likely to have their
homes broken into or to be robbed on their way to work than
they would be in an irreligious society, because of the powerful deterrent effects of religion on crime. Moreover, religious
people are the primary source of secular charitable funds that
benefit all victims of misfortune whatever their beliefs. Indeed,

religious people dominate the ranks of blood donors, to whom even some angry humanists owe their lives.

It is past time for a full accounting of the tangible human and social benefits of faith in American society and for the recognition that one of our nation's primary advantages over many others lies in the greater strength of religion in American life. As will be seen, this accounting is surprisingly easy because mountains of little-reported research and reliable data exist on a wide range of important religious effects. For example, *compared to less religious and irreligious Americans,*

- ▶ At all ages, religious people are much less likely to commit crimes.

- ▶ Religious Americans are far more likely to contribute even to secular charities, to volunteer their time to socially beneficial programs, and to be active in civic affairs.

- ▶ Religious Americans enjoy superior mental health—they are happier, less neurotic, and far less likely to commit suicide.

- ▶ Religious Americans also enjoy superior physical health, having an average life expectancy more than seven years longer than that of the irreligious. A very substantial difference remains even after the effects of "clean living" are removed.

- ▶ Religious people are more apt to marry and less likely to divorce, and they express higher degrees of satisfaction with their spouses. They also are more likely to have children.

- ▶ Religious husbands are substantially less likely to abuse their wives or children.

- ▶ Religious American couples enjoy their sex lives more and are far less likely to have extramarital affairs.

- ▶ Religious students perform better on standardized achievement tests.

- ▶ Religious Americans are far less likely to have dropped out of school, which is especially true for African Americans and Hispanics.

- ► Religious Americans are more successful, obtaining better jobs and far less subject to being on unemployment or welfare; this is true not only for whites but for African Americans.
- ► Although often portrayed as ignorant philistines, religious Americans are more likely to consume and sustain "high culture."
- ► Religious people are far less likely to believe in occult and paranormal phenomena such as Bigfoot, UFOs, Atlantis, ghosts, haunted houses, and astrology.

Translated into comparisons with Western European nations, we enjoy far lower crime rates, much higher levels of charitable giving, better health, stronger marriages, and less suicide, to note only a few of our benefits from being an unusually religious nation. Quite aside from the social and personal benefits of these religious effects, they add up to many hundreds of billions of dollars a year in financial benefits, as I demonstrate in the concluding chapter.

Unfortunately, many of these benefits have been disparaged or even denied, especially by academics. For example, as reported in chapter 5, it remains an article of faith among most psychologists that religion either contributes to mental illness or is itself a form of psychopathology, although the evidence shows overwhelmingly that religion protects against mental illness. In similar fashion, chapter 3 notes that many social scientists continue to claim that Evangelical Protestant husbands are wife beaters, despite a mountain of contrary research studies. And so it goes. But far more significant even than denial is simple neglect. For example, despite several hundred studies demonstrating strong religious effects on obeying the law, the word "religion" does not even appear in the index of fourteen of sixteen leading textbooks on criminology.

Some might suppose that this neglect of religious benefits is partly due to the fact that religion is rapidly declining even in America, and therefore its role in these matters lacks long-term significance. On March 17, 2009, *USA Today* ran a story headlined "Most Religious Groups in USA Have Lost Ground." A month later the lead story in *Newsweek* announced "The End of Christian America." Nonsense. Despite these frequent media claims, American religion is not declining. To the contrary, more Americans (70 percent) now belong to a local church congregation than ever before in our history.

Of course, a major reason for the neglect of religious benefits is the growing antagonism toward religion so carefully promulgated by the news media. Increasingly, zoning officials are preventing the construction of new churches and are prosecuting people who host small Bible-study groups weekly in their homes and who lack (unobtainable) licenses to hold public meetings. In addition, it has become fashionable to complain about religious buildings being exempt from property taxes and for religious contributions to be deductible. Some now suggest that these are forms of favoritism that violate the separation of church and state. But the underlying motivation for these complaints has far less to do with concerns about traffic, the need to increase government revenues, or interpreting the First Amendment than with contempt for religion and antagonism toward religious people.

Recently, in an article in the online edition of *The Atlantic* about former Arkansas governor and Fox Media host Mike Huckabee, associate editor Nicole Allan noted that "people are sometimes caught off guard by Huckabee's intellectual competence because of . . . his outspoken evangelical views."[2] This remark reflects the prevailing view among journalists, openly stated by the prominent Michael Weisskopf in the *Washington Post*, that Evangelical Protestants are "poor, uneducated and easy to command."[3] Media people are ignorant of the fact that the better educated they are, the more frequently Americans attend church,[4] probably because no one they know is religious.[5] A few years ago, a survey of journalists randomly selected from the most influential news organizations (the major TV networks, *Time*, *Newsweek*, the *New York Times*, *Washington Post*, and the like) found that 50 percent listed their religion as "none" (for emphasis, some carefully underlined it) and 86 percent said they seldom or never went to church.[6]

I can't explain why there are so few religious people among journalists, but that has been the case for a long time. Except for his remarkable talent, H. L. Mencken (1880–1956) probably was not an oddity; most of his newsroom colleagues probably scoffed at religion, too. That certainly was how things were back when I was a writer for several major newspapers. If anything has changed since then, it would be that even fewer media people are religious, and those who are usually keep it to themselves. The lack of religious people in the media environment not only breeds contempt ("Smart people like us aren't religious") but also leads to invincible ignorance. For example, the idea that deeply religious couples have more active and satisfying sex lives than do the irreligious is simply inconceivable to elite media people, the majority of whom do not believe that adultery is wrong.[7]

In what follows I make no claims that are not backed by good research studies or reliable data. What do I mean by good research? The primary factor in good social research has to do with sampling. For every published social scientific study based on a random sample of a relevant population, at least a dozen are based on accidental collections of people such as 142 students in an introductory psychology class at some junior college, or a random sample of a very unrepresentative population such as tattooed residents of Waco, Texas. It is impossible to place confidence in any nonexperimental research based on a grab bag of respondents, which is why the findings from such studies differ so wildly—from reports that all churchgoing coeds are virgins to reports that there is not a virgin among them. I exclude all studies not based on well-selected samples of relevant populations, making only a few exceptions that I am careful to point out and justify.

Beyond sampling is analysis. Suppose a study of a well-selected national sample of teenagers reported that those who attend church are less likely to have shoplifted. But we know that girls are significantly less likely than boys to shoplift and girls also are more likely to attend church. So, is the initial finding a real religious effect, or is it the case that gender differences are masquerading as a religious effect? That is, when the relationship between church attendance and shoplifting is examined separately for boys and girls, is there still a religious effect? Yes, there is. Among both boys and girls, those who are religious are less likely to shoplift. That is an example of analysis. I only report studies that meet professional standards of analysis. In some instances, I present reliable data that no one has bothered to use to sustain an important point about the role of religion. In those instances, I also take the necessary analytic precautions.

Acknowledgments

Usually, I am a rather solitary scholar. But in this instance I enjoyed invaluable help from my colleagues at Baylor's Institute for Studies of Religion. Byron Johnson offered continuing advice and kept the world at bay. Jeff Levin shared his encyclopedic knowledge of the effects of religion on psychological and physical health. Young-Il Kim helped me deal with various data sets, including the enormous Gallup World Polls. And Frances Malone secured for me copies of studies published in various hard-to-get journals.

Thank you.

* 1 *

Creating Religious America

M OST PEOPLE probably believe that Colonial America was
far more religious than the nation is today—their impres-
sions strongly shaped by pictures of Puritans dressed in somber
clothing on their way to church. But most colonists were not
Puritans; Puritans were not even a majority of those aboard
the *Mayflower*. In 1776 the overwhelming majority of colonists
in America did not even belong to a local church. Only about
17 percent did so, and even in New England only 22 percent
belonged.[1] As for the somber Puritans, they wore plain, drab
clothing only on Sunday. On other days they tended to favor
bright colors. Those who "could afford it wore crimson waist-
coats and expensive cloaks,"[2] and the women wore jewelry and
very fancy clothing at appropriate times. Moreover, from 1761
through 1800, a third (33.7 percent) of all first births in New
England occurred after less than nine months of marriage, so
single women in Colonial New England were more likely to
engage in premarital sex than to attend church.[3]

The very low level of religious participation that existed in
the thirteen colonies merely reflected that the settlers brought
with them the low level that prevailed in Europe. Then, as now,
the monopoly state churches of Europe, fully supported by taxes
and therefore having no need to arouse public support, were
very poorly attended. This situation was not a new develop-
ment. Contrary to another popular myth, medieval Europeans

seldom went to church and were, at most, barely Christian.[4]
That state of affairs was not changed by the Reformation, which
simply replaced poorly attended Catholic churches with poorly
attended Protestant monopoly state churches.

In addition, some of the larger Colonial denominations, such
as the Episcopalians and Lutherans, were overseas branches of
state churches and not only displayed the lack of effort typical
of such establishments but were also remarkable for sending
disreputable clergy to minister to the colonies. As the celebrated
Edwin S. Gaustad noted, there was constant grumbling by Episcopalian (Anglican) vestrymen "about clergy that left England
to escape debts or wives or onerous duties, seeing [America] as
a place of retirement or refuge."[5] The great Colonial evangelist
George Whitefield noted in his journal that it would be better
"that people had no minister than such as are generally sent
over . . . who, for the most part, lead very bad examples."[6]

In addition, most colonies suffered from having a legally
established denomination, supported by taxes. The Episcopalians were the established church in New York, Virginia,
Maryland, North Carolina, South Carolina, and Georgia. The
Congregationalists (Puritans) were established in New England.
There was no established church in New Jersey or Pennsylvania,
and not surprisingly these two colonies had higher membership
rates than did any other colony.[7]

Therein lies a clue as to the rise of the amazing levels of
American piety: competition creates energetic churches. As
Adam Smith explained in 1776, established religions, being
monopolies, inevitably are lax and lazy. In contrast, according
to Smith, clergy who must depend upon their members for support usually exhibit far greater "zeal and industry" than those
who are provided for by law. History is full of examples wherein
a kept clergy "reposing themselves upon their benefices, had
neglected to keep up the fervour of faith and devotion in the
great body of the people; and having given themselves up to

indolence, were become altogether incapable of making any vigorous defence even of their own establishment." Smith went on to note that the clergy of monopoly churches often become "men of learning and elegance," but they have "no other resource than to call upon the civil magistrate to persecute, destroy, or drive out their adversaries."[8] Smith's claims were fully demonstrated by the weakness of European Christianity. But the lazy colonial monopolies did not survive in the United States, being replaced by a religious free market in which Smith's analysis was fully confirmed.

PLURALISM AND PIETY

Following the Revolutionary War, state religious establishments were discontinued (although the Congregationalists held on as the established church of Massachusetts until 1833), and even in 1776 there was substantial pluralism building up everywhere. This increased rapidly with the appearance of many new Protestant sects—most of them of local origins. With all of these denominations placed on an equal footing, intense competition arose among the churches for member support, and the net result of their combined efforts was a dramatic increase in Americans' religious participation. By 1850 a third of Americans belonged to a local congregation. By the start of the twentieth century, half of Americans belonged, and today about 70 percent are affiliated with a local church.[9]

From the early days, people generally knew that competitive pluralism accounted for the increasingly great differences in the piety of Americans and Europeans. The German nobleman Francis Grund, who arrived in Boston in 1827, noted that establishment makes the clergy "indolent and Lazy," because

> a person provided for cannot, by the rules of common sense, be supposed to work as hard as once who

has to exert himself for a living. . . . Not only have
Americans a greater number of clergymen than, in
proportion to the population, can be found on the
Continent or in England; but they have not one idler
amongst them; all of them being obliged to exert
themselves for the spiritual welfare of their respec-
tive congregations. The Americans, therefore, enjoy a
three-fold advantage: they have more preachers; they
have more active preachers, and they have cheaper
preachers than can be found in any part of Europe.[10]

Another German, the militant atheist Karl T. Griesinger,
complained in 1852 that the separation of church and state in
America fueled religious efforts: "Clergymen in America [are]
like other businessmen; they must meet competition and build
up a trade. . . . Now it is clear . . . why attendance is more common here than anywhere else in the world."[11]

But competition did not benefit all of the American denominations, as can be seen in Table 1.1; some were unable (or
unwilling) to compete. It would be very misleading to compute
market shares in 1776 and 1850 as a percentage of church members since the rate of church membership precisely doubled
during this period. This problem is eliminated by basing market shares on the entire population, churched and unchurched.
That also takes into account the rapid growth of the population
during this same period. When population growth is ignored,
all denominations appear to have been quite successful; even
the Congregationalists nearly trebled their numbers, and the
Episcopalians more than did so. But when market shares are
examined, it becomes obvious that the Congregationalists and
Episcopalians had suffered catastrophic losses. The Presbyterians had held their own. The Baptists had made an immense gain
(from 29 per 1,000 to 70), and the Methodists had achieved an

incredible share of the religious marketplace, going from 2 per 1,000 to 116. During this era the Roman Catholics grew, too.

TABLE 1.1. CHURCH MEMBERSHIP, 1776–1850

	1776		1850	
	Total Membership*	Per 1,000 Population**	Total Membership*	Per 1,000 Population**
Congregational	83,800	34	315,400	14
Episcopal	64,500	27	275,900	12
Presbyterian	78,100	32	914,600	39
Baptist	69,400	29	1,616,400	70
Methodist	4,900	2	2,696,700	116
Roman Catholic	7,400	3	1,096,000	47
All religious groups	411,000	170	7,885,200	340

* rounded to nearest 100
** rounded to nearest whole number

Source: Calculated from Finke and Stark 1992

Pluralism Misconceived

Oddly, the recognition that competition among religious groups was the dynamic behind the ever-rising levels of American religious participation withered away in the twentieth century as social scientists began to reassert the charges long leveled against pluralism by monopoly religions: that disputes among religious groups undercut the credibility of all, hence religion is strongest where it enjoys an unchallenged monopoly. This view was formulated into elegant sociology by the prominent sociologist Peter Berger, who repeatedly argued that pluralism inevitably destroys the plausibility of all religions because only where a single faith prevails can there exist a "sacred canopy" that spreads a common outlook over an entire society, inspiring universal confidence and assent. As Berger explained, "the classical task of religion" is to construct "a common world within which all of social life receives ultimate meaning binding on everybody."[12] Thus, by ignoring the stunning evidence of American history, Berger and his many supporters concluded that religion was doomed by pluralism, and that to survive, therefore, modern societies would need to develop new, secular canopies.

But Berger was quite wrong, as even he eventually admitted very gracefully.[13] It seems to be the case that people don't need all-embracing sacred canopies, but are sufficiently served by "sacred umbrellas," to use Christian Smith's wonderful image.[14] Smith explained that people don't need to agree with all their neighbors in order to sustain their religious convictions, they only need a set of like-minded friends; pluralism does not challenge the credibility of religions because groups can be entirely committed to their faith despite the presence of others committed to another. Thus, in a study of Catholic charismatics, Mary Jo Neitz found their full awareness of religious choices "did not undermine their own beliefs. Rather they felt they had 'tested' the belief system and been convinced of its superiority."[15] And in her study of secular Jewish women who converted to Orthodoxy, Lynn Davidman stressed how the "pluralization and multiplicity of choices available in the contemporary United States can actually strengthen Jewish communities."[16] A national survey conducted in 1999 found that 40 percent of Americans have "shopped around" before selecting their present church, and these shoppers have a higher rate of attendance than do those who did not shop.[17]

The Poverty of Permissive Religion

But if they have been forced to retreat from the charge that pluralism is incompatible with faith, critics of pluralism now advance spurious notions about the consequences of competition for religious authenticity. The new claim is that competition must force religious groups to become more permissive—that in an effort to attract supporters, churches will be forced to vie with one another to offer less demanding faiths, to ask for less in the way of member sacrifices and levels of commitment. Here, too, it was Peter Berger who made the point first, and most effectively. Competition among American faiths, he wrote, has placed all churches at the mercy of "consumer preference."[18] Consumers prefer "religious products that can be made consonant with secularized consciousness. . . . Religious contents . . . modified in a secularizing direction . . . may lead to a deliberate excision of all or nearly all 'supernatural' elements from the religious tradition . . . [or] it may just mean that the 'supernatural' elements are de-emphasized or pushed into the background, while the institution is 'sold' under the label of values congenial to secularized consciousness."[19] If so, then the successful churches will be those that minimize the need to accept miraculous, supernatural elements of faith, that impose few moral requirements, and which are content with minimal levels of participation and support. In this way, pluralism leads to the ruination of traditional religion. Thus did Oxford's Bryan Wilson dismiss the vigor of American religion on grounds of "the generally accepted superficiality of much religion in American society,"[20] smugly presuming that somehow greater depth was being achieved in the empty churches of Britain and the Continent. In similar fashion, John Burdick proposed that competition among religions reduces their offerings to "purely opportunistic efforts."[21] But it's not so. The conclusion that competition among faiths will favor "cheap" religious organizations mistakes price for value. As is evident in most consumer markets, people do not usually rush to purchase the cheapest model or variety, but attempt to maximize by selecting the item that offers the most for their money—that offers the best value. In the case of religion, people do not flock to faiths that ask the least of them, but to those that credibly offer the most religious rewards for the sacrifices required to qualify.

FROM MAINLINE TO SIDELINE

Not so many years ago, a select set of American denominations was always referred to as the Protestant "mainline": the Congregationalists, Episcopalians, Presbyterians, Methodists, American Baptists, Christian Church (Disciples of Christ), and, more recently, the Evangelical Lutherans. As the name "mainline" suggests, these denominations had such social cachet that when Americans rose to prominence they often shed their old religious affiliation and joined one of these bodies. Today, although media bias and ignorance often result in these groups still being identified as the mainline, that designation is very much out of date; the old mainline has rapidly faded to the religious periphery, a trend first noticed about forty years ago.

In 1972 Dean M. Kelley, a Methodist clergyman and an executive of the National Council of Churches, provoked a storm of criticism by pointing out a most unwelcome fact: "In the latter years of the 1960s something remarkable happened in the United States: for the first time in the nation's history most of the major church groups stopped growing and began to shrink."[22] Kelley was being somewhat diplomatic when he referred to "most . . . major church groups," knowing full well that the decline was limited to the mainline Protestant bodies.

Kelley's book stirred up angry and bitter denials. Writing in the *Christian Century*, Carl Bangs[23] accused him of using deceptive statistics, even though Kelley had relied entirely on the official statistics reported by each denomination. Everett L. Perry, research director of the Presbyterian Church, called Kelley an ideologue who "marshaled data . . . to support his point of view."[24] Martin E. Marty dismissed the declines as but a momentary reflection of the "cultural crisis" of the sixties.[25] If so, then the declines should have been momentary as well. In fact, the declines accelerated, as can be seen in Table 1.2.

As with Table 1.1, in order to eliminate the effects of population growth, in Table 1.2 denominational size is calculated as the number of members per 1,000 Americans, which can be interpreted as each denomination's market share. Each of these seven denominations in Table 1.2 has suffered catastrophic declines; most have lost more than half of their 1960 market share, some of them far more. To make matters worse, all of these denominations suffer from having very elderly congregations, presaging an even more rapid decline.

TABLE 1.2. THE DECLINING "MAINLINE"
(U.S. Members per 1,000 U.S. Population)

Denomination	1960	1970	2000	2010
United Church of Christ (formerly Congregationalist)	12.4	9.6	4.9	3.2
Episcopal	18.1	16.1	8.2	6.1
Presbyterian USA	23.0	19.8	12.7	8.7
United Methodist	54.7	51.6	29.7	24.9
American Baptist USA	8.6	7.7	5.2	4.2
Christian Church (Disciples of Christ)	6.2	6.1	3.8	2.0
Evangelical Lutheran Church in America	29.3	27.7	18.2	13.6

Source: Yearbook of the American and Canadian Churches, appropriate editions.

Some have dismissed these declines as merely reflecting a more general decline in the nation's religiousness, claiming that America finally has begun to follow Europe along the road to irreligion. Not so. Americans remain just as likely to attend church as they ever did, and more Americans now belong to a local church than ever before.[26] Others have shrugged off these declines as merely reflecting a drop in the relative number of Protestants in response to high rates of Catholic immigration. But that excuse fails because the Catholic market share has declined slightly since 1960.

If the data in Table 1.2 were all we had to go on, the debate as to why these declines occurred might be irresolvable. But Kelley did not merely claim that the mainline was declining; he pointed out that the conservative churches were more than taking up the slack. In fact, Kelley headlined this contrast in the title of his book, *Why Conservative Churches Are Growing*. That's really what riled academics and mainline clergy.

Some dismissed conservative growth as nothing more than fraudulent statistics. Others admitted that the membership roles kept by the conservative churches were honest, but claimed they were greatly inflated because so many of their members hop from church to church that they get counted two or three times.[27] Several have argued that the growth of conservative churches is primarily due to higher levels of fertility among their members, in contrast with the very low fertility of the mainline.[28] But this mostly reflects that the mainline congregations grew old and therefore currently lack fertility, because the sons and daughters of the remaining members defected and took their fertility with them. It has been suggested that the growth of conservative Protestant denominations merely reflects the growth of the South.[29] But the declines have occurred in every region. The significant fact that overwhelms all objections is that most who join conservative churches as adults grew up in mainline churches.[30] Finally, many liberals have even attempted to make a virtue of the mainline decline, claiming that the contrasting trends reflect the superior moral worth of the mainline—that if the conservative churches are growing it is because they are "herding insecure and frightened masses together into a superficial conformity," while the mainline churches remain as a "faithful remnant of God's people whose prophetic courage and lifestyle truly point the way."[31] Meanwhile, the mainline continues to shrink, and the conservative churches continue to grow.

As shown in Table 1.3, since 1960 many conservative religious groups have been gaining members at a remarkably rapid rate; many have trebled in size. As a result, the Assemblies of God is now larger than the combined total of Congregationalists and American Baptists, more than four times as large as the Christian Church, larger than the Episcopalians, and as large as the Presbyterians (USA). The Pentecostal Assemblies of the World has surpassed the Congregationalists, the American Baptists, and the Christian Church. There are more Mormons than Evangelical Lutherans, and they soon will pass the Methodists. There are as many Jehovah's Witnesses as there are Congregationalists. Nevertheless, the growth of all of these conservative bodies is dwarfed by the number of Americans who have joined nondenominational, evangelical, Protestant congregations—people who often give their religious affiliation as "Christian." In 1960 there were very few such congregations. Today they enroll more members than do the Methodists and more than half as many as do the Southern Baptists. In fact, the growth of the nondenominational evangelical churches accounts for the slight recent decline in the Southern Baptist market share.

Many have asked why millions of Americans left the denominations in which they were raised for a more conservative church. But the more appropriate question is why did the leaders of the old Protestant mainline denominations knowingly drive away so many members? *How* they did so is not difficult to discover. As Jeffrey K. Hadden wrote in *The Gathering Storm*

TABLE 1.3. SOME GROWING DENOMINATIONS
(U.S. Members per 1,000 U.S. Population)

Denomination	1960	2010
Latter-Day Saints (Mormons)	8.2	20.0
Assemblies of God	2.8	9.7
Pentecostal Assemblies of the World	0.2	5.8
Jehovah's Witnesses	1.3	3.8
Seventh-day Adventists	1.8	3.6
Church of God (Cleveland, Tenn.)	0.9	3.6
United Pentecostal Church International	0.7	2.5
Nondenominational Evangelical Protestant Congregations	few	34.8*
Southern Baptist Convention	53.8	52.6

*Pew Forum Survey 2007.

Source: Yearbook of the American and Canadian Churches, appropriate editions.

in the Churches back in 1969, over the years a huge gap opened between the mainline clergy and the people in their pews. This gap had two primary features: clergy disbelief in the essentials of Christianity, and the clergy's unquestioned faith in radical politics.

THEOLOGIES OF DOUBT AND DENIAL

The wreckage of the former mainline denominations is strewn upon the shoal of a modernist theology that began to dominate the mainline seminaries early in the nineteenth century, based on the presumption that advances in human knowledge had made faith outmoded. If religion was to survive it must become "modern and progressive and . . . the meaning of Christianity should be interpreted from the standpoint of modern knowledge and experience."[32] From this starting point, science soon took precedence over revelation, and the spiritual realm faded into psychology. Eventually, mainline theologians discarded nearly every doctrinal aspect of traditional Christianity. Sketches of several of the major figures can clarify this claim.

One of the first leaders in this shift toward theologies of doubt and denial was William Ellery Channing (1760–1842), a Harvard graduate and Boston minister who became the most celebrated preacher of his era. Channing taught that most traditional Christian beliefs were "suited perhaps to darker ages. But they have done their work and should pass away. Christianity should now be disencumbered and set free from unintelligible and traditional doctrines, and the uncouth and idolatrous forms and ceremonies, which terror, superstition, vanity, priestcraft and ambition have laboured to identify with it."[33] A long line of celebrated theologians followed Channing, all echoing his message.

In 1912 William Ernest Hocking (1873–1966), a Harvard theologian, published a book nearly six hundred pages long devoted to developing his conception of God: *The Meaning of God in Human Experience*. Despite the fact that Hocking constantly assured his readers that God does exist, by the end of the book it remained quite uncertain what Hocking meant by "exist," let alone by "God." He made it clear enough that he rejected the traditional Christian conception of God as a conscious, active being or entity. But nowhere did he define the God in whom he "believed" in other than metaphorical language. As Hocking repeatedly put it, God is "Other Mind,"[34] "our Absolute Other,"[35] or God is "the unity of human nature."[36] Given his claim that even most atheists could accept his "God," Hocking must have been fully aware that these phrases were so vague as to be meaningless. Hocking wasn't merely a Harvard professor; he was a prominent public figure, often written up in the major newspapers and magazines. What he taught subsequent generations of mainline theologians was how to say they believed in God and not mean it.

And, finally, Paul Tillich (1886–1965): Despite the fact that Tillich's theology and especially his definition of God are fundamentally incomprehensible, or perhaps because they are, he has had more lasting impact on the beliefs of contemporary mainline clergy than anyone else. To look him up online is to confront hundreds of entries hailing him as the leading theologian of the twentieth century and, by implication, of all time. The logical inadequacy and spurious profundity of Tillich's theology would seem to be obvious to an unbiased reader.[37] But few read him without first having been assured that they are reading a profound thinker and thus they suppose that something deeply meaningful must underlie passages such as this one: "Faith is a total and centered act of the personal self, the act of unconditional, infinite, and ultimate concern. . . . The unconditional concern which is faith is the concern about the unconditional. The infinite passion, as faith has been described, is the passion for the infinite. Or, to use our first term, the ultimate concern is concern about what is experienced as ultimate."[38] Regardless of authorship, these are empty tautologies. Herein lies the secret of the immense prestige and influence of Tillich and the other liberal theologians. Their convoluted prose earned them a reputation for profundity while very successfully obscuring their lack of Christian faith.

Thus, Tillich devoted hundreds of pages to asserting his belief in God. But what did he mean by the word "God"? Surely not God the Father almighty, maker of heaven and earth. He condemned that God as an "invincible tyrant, the being in contrast with whom all other beings are without freedom . . . He is equated with recent tyrants who with the help of terror try to transform everything into . . . a cog in the machine they control. . . . This is the God Nietzsche said had to be killed because nobody can tolerate being made into a mere object of absolute knowledge and absolute control. This is the deepest root of atheism. It is an atheism which is justified as the reaction against theological theism and its disturbing implications."[39]

Thus, in Tillich's view, God is not a being and to claim otherwise is to "relapse into monarchic monotheism."[40] Indeed, "God does not exist. He is being itself beyond essence and existence."[41] God is "the ground of being."[42] The key question is what does this phrase mean? "God as being-itself is the ground of the ontological structure of being without being subject to this structure himself. . . . Therefore, if anything beyond this base assertion is said about God, it no longer is a direct and proper statement, no longer a concept. It is indirect, and it points to something beyond itself. In a word, it is symbolic."[43] But if God is strictly defined as being-itself, and being-itself has only symbolic meaning, then Tillich's God is merely symbolic.[44]

It is obviously as pointless to worship Tillich's God as it is to worship God as defined by most of the other twentieth-century mainline theologians. How can clergy who reject a God who sees, hears, or cares in good conscience conduct a worship service? One could as effectively pray to any stone idol. And, of course, through the years many people in the pews recognized this charade as they caught a glimpse of their pastor's lack of belief in a personal God—a phenomenon that had become widespread among the clergy because it had come to dominate the mainline seminaries.

Thus, a survey study of local pastors conducted in 1968 revealed that a substantial proportion of mainline clergy were unwilling to express certainty in the existence of God or the divinity of Jesus.[45] Subsequently John Shelby Spong, the most prolific author of atheist books during the past several decades, served as an Episcopalian bishop until his recent retirement.

Under his leadership, his diocese in New Jersey lost more than 40 percent of its members, compared with a 16 percent decline in the Episcopal Church as a whole during these years.[46] Even though so many have left, most of the people remaining in the former mainline pews still regard the traditional tenets of Christianity as central to their faith, hence the exodus continues—now often involving entire congregations.

Radical Leftists

Hand in hand with theologies of doubt and disbelief came certainty in the virtues of the socialist revolution. In 1934 a national survey of nearly twenty thousand mainline clergy found that when asked, "Which economic system appears to you to be less antagonistic to and more consistent with the ideals and methods of Jesus and the noblest of the Hebrew prophets? Capitalism or a Cooperative Commonwealth?" 5 percent opted for capitalism and 87 percent for a cooperative commonwealth, which everyone understood to mean socialism.[47] This was entirely consistent with the formal resolutions of the Federal Council of Churches (FCC), an association that had been formed by the mainline churches in 1908. In fact, the founding "creed" of the FCC called for the reduction of the workday "to the lowest practicable point," for the "highest wage that each industry can afford," "for the abatement of poverty," "for the most equitable division of the products of industry that can ultimately be devised," and so on. The creed set a pattern for future statements by the Council that nearly always involved "outspoken liberal advocacy," as Yale historian Sydney Ahlstrom (1919–1984) put it.[48] For example, in its annual report for 1930 the Federal Council noted that "the Christian ideal calls for hearty support for a planned economic system in which maximum social values shall be brought. It demands that cooperation shall supplant competition as the fundamental method."[49] Again, everyone involved regarded this as a call for socialism.

Consider this astonishing example of the open commitment of the mainline clergy to socialism in this era: three days after the fall of France to the Nazi blitzkrieg in 1940, the editors of *Christian Century*—then as now the most influential mainline Protestant publication—solemnly pondered whether Hitler could be trusted to remain committed to "social revolution . . . of which he has been the prophet and leader in Germany . . . [Will he continue to reject] Capitalist imperialism?" they asked.[50] This uncritical left-wing commitment was continued by the National Council of Churches (NCC), as the Federal Council renamed itself in 1950. The new name changed nothing. Although the NCC (and the mainline clergy in general) has avoided open use of the term "socialism," the commitment to a radical redistribution of wealth and antagonism toward capitalism has continued without pause. Frequent, too, are the expressions of support for the Castro regime in Cuba. Attacks on Israel and commendations of the Palestinians are emitted with regularity. The NCC has claimed that the primary purpose of the American criminal justice system has nothing to do with crime, but with the repression of dissent. Condemnations have been issued against homeschooling and public Christmas displays. And on and on. Aware that most members reject their radical political views, the mainline clergy claim it is their right and duty to instruct the faithful in more sophisticated and enlightened religious and political views. So every year thousands of members claim their right to leave. And, of course, in the very pluralistic and competitive American religious marketplace, many appealing alternatives are available.

Has rapidly falling membership caused second thoughts among the prominent mainline clergy, among faculty at the famous divinity schools, or in the headquarters of the National Council of Churches on Riverside Drive in Manhattan? Not for a minute. Instead, the gap Hadden noted has continued to grow and membership has continued to shrink, until recently large, organized, dissenting groups have begun departing en masse. As the Methodist theologian and Duke Divinity School professor Stanley Hauerwas explained, "God is killing mainline Protestantism in America, and we goddam well deserve it."[51]

Catholic and Jewish Examples

The decline of the liberal Protestant churches and the growth of more conservative Protestantism is in keeping with recent changes within both Roman Catholicism and Judaism.

Among the many actions taken at the Second Vatican Council meetings of the Roman Catholic Church held during the early to mid-1960s were some that greatly reduced the sacrifices required of nuns and monks. For example, many orders of nuns were allowed to abandon their elaborate garb and wear clothing that does not identify them as members of a religious order. Other Vatican II actions revoked rules requiring many hours of daily prayer and meditation in convents and monasteries. These and many similar "reforms" were widely hailed as inaugurating a worldwide renewal of the religious orders by making the religious life less "costly." Within a year, a rapid decline ensued. Many nuns and monks withdrew from their orders. Entry rates plummeted. The orders shrank. Thus, the number of nuns in the United States fell from 176,671 in 1966, when the Council adjourned, to 71,487 in 2004, and the number of monks fell by half. Similar declines took place around the world. These declines have nearly always been explained (usually by ex-nuns who now are professors of sociology)[52] as the result of continuing to place too-severe demands upon members of the orders—demands incompatible with modern life. But what is truly revealing is that the process has turned out to be reversible. Some religious orders reinstated the old requirements, and some new orders were founded that again ask for high levels of sacrifice. These orders have been growing.[53] So much for the claims that the levels of sacrifice were too high.

As an additional example, it has long been recognized that the market share of Orthodox Jewish congregations has been growing while Reform Judaism has been in decline. For years this was attributed entirely to fertility differences: the Orthodox have high fertility, other Jews have very low fertility. But recently, observers have begun to recognize that a significant portion of the Orthodox growth is due to an influx of new members from the ranks of the less-demanding Jewish bodies and, indeed, from the conversion of large numbers of secular Jews, unaffiliated with any synagogue.[54] In response, many Reform synagogues have restored some of the more demanding Orthodox practices.[55]

RELIGIOUS AMERICA

Including members of Jewish synagogues, about seven in ten Americans belong to a religious congregation. On an ordinary Sabbath, nearly half of Americans are in church and nearly half of the population (49 percent) pray at least once each day. A fourth (28 percent) read the Bible weekly. About a third (31 percent) consider themselves to be "very religious," and another 42 percent say they are "somewhat religious." As for heaven, 62 percent are "absolutely" sure it exists, while another 20 percent think it "probably" exists. Eighty-two percent of Americans believe in angels, and 55 percent claim, "I was protected from harm by a guardian angel."[56] Clearly, this nation is very religious. That hasn't prevented some from eagerly claiming that American religion is rapidly declining.

"No Religion"

Most recently the media have widely trumpeted the claim that American religion is finally ebbing away and America is soon to become secularized. In a press release issued early in March 2009 the director of the American Religious Identification Survey (ARIS) reported that 15 percent of Americans responding to a brief telephone interview selected the "no religion" response when asked their religious preference. This was almost double the 8 percent who gave that response to a similar poll in 1990. The press release revealing these results also stressed that the mainline Christian denominations had suffered substantial declines over the same period.

This announcement produced ecstatic reactions on the atheist websites as well as a huge response in the national media. One *USA Today* story carried the headline, "Most Religious Groups in USA Have Lost Ground, Survey Finds."[57] Jon Meacham, then editor of *Newsweek*, wrote a lead story, "The End of Christian America."[58] (No, there was no question mark.) But anyone without an axe to grind and with minimal knowledge of poll data on American religion knew that these conclusions were absurd; the real meaning of the "no religion" response had been carefully omitted from the press release, and as we have seen, the decline of the mainline denominations has been going on for generations and is offset by the rise of more conservative bodies.

An extensive research literature shows that the great majority of Americans who respond that they have "no religion" are not atheists (as the ARIS press release implied) but are quite religious. Although "no religion" is the answer that the 3 or 4 percent of Americans who profess atheism give to pollsters, most people who give this response seem to mean only that they *do not belong to a church*. Thus, recent studies[59] have found that more than 90 percent of them pray, and 39 percent pray weekly or more often. Only 14 percent do not believe in God, and half of them believe in angels. As might be expected of people who seldom attend any church, some of their beliefs are not very orthodox. For example, 18 percent define their God as some sort of higher power or cosmic force. Forty-five percent believe that astrology is true, and another 8 percent think it could be true.

Half of those who say they have "no religion" frequent New Age bookstores, and they are especially prone to believe in ghosts, Bigfoot, and Atlantis.[60] There may be some basis for disputing whether such people are Christians, but it is beyond question that they are religious.

The ARIS press release also failed to note that the percentage of Americans who actually belong to a local church congregation has continued to rise over this same period, from 64 percent in 1990 to about 70 percent in 2007. Finally, although the press release suggested otherwise, the percentage of Americans who are atheists hasn't changed in the past sixty years. Four percent told the Gallup Poll in 1944 that they did not believe in God, exactly the same percentage as in the Baylor National Survey of Religion in 2007.

European Religious Apathy

This chapter began by noting that religiousness has always been rather low in Western Europe, or at least lower than in the United States. That remains true, as is shown in Table 1.4. Church attendance is substantially lower in every Western European nation (for which current rates were available), with the exception of Italy, where 31 percent report being weekly church attenders, compared with 36 percent in the United States—many other Americans claim to attend nearly every week. Italy is an interesting exception, not because the Vatican is located in Rome, but because a change in the tax laws resulted in a religious free market that has produced a religious revival.[61] In contrast, church attendance in Scandinavia is minuscule.

Europeans, even Italians, are far less likely than Americans to say that God is very important in their lives, which may be more reflective of trans-Atlantic religious differences than is church attendance. On the other hand, although Americans are more likely to believe in life after death (81 percent) than are Europe-

TABLE 1.4. AMERICAN RELIGIOUSNESS COMPARED WITH WESTERN EUROPE

	Attend Church Weekly	Importance of God**	Believe in Life after Death**
United States	36%	65%	81%
Italy	31%	47%	72%
Austria**	23%	34%	59%
United Kingdom	17%	27%	58%
Belgium**	17%	19%	43%
Spain	16%	17%	53%
Greece	14%	42%	61%
Switzerland	12%	31%	64%
Netherlands	12%	15%	51%
Germany	8%	15%	30%
France	7%	14%	45%
Finland	7%	26%	56%
Norway	4%	14%	47%
Denmark**	3%	9%	38%
Sweden	3%	11%	46%

* "How important is God in your life?" On a scale of 1 through 10, combined scores of 9 and 10.

** World Values Surveys 1999–2000.

Source: World Values Surveys 2005–2008

ans, in most of these nations the majority do believe, and even in Denmark more than a third do so.

The question arises as to why Europeans are so much less religious than are Americans. I have pursued this question at length in a recent book,[62] and the explanation begins with the Emperor Constantine's (275–337) meddling in church affairs.

However, it is sufficient here to focus on present matters that *keep* European churches so empty.

Monopoly Churches

In most European nations there is nothing resembling a religious free market. Many countries have established state churches supported by taxes. In most of the rest, a particular church is the object of considerable government favoritism. And in nearly all European nations, the government bureaucracy engages in overt and covert interference with all religious outsiders and newcomers that challenge the established religious order. State churches have long dominated European religion. For centuries the Catholic Church imposed a monopoly; the Reformation initiated Protestant monopolies. Control of religion, of course, suits the preference of many European governments to control all important social institutions.

These close links between church and state have many consequences. First of all, they create lazy churches. Being supported by taxes, the money continues to come whether people attend or not, so that there is no need for clergy to exert themselves. Second, these links encourage people to view religion "as a type of public utility."[63] Individuals need do nothing to preserve the church; the government will see to it. This attitude makes it difficult for nonsubsidized faiths to compete, and people are reluctant to contribute to a church. Thus, when some German evangelists attempted television ministries, they drew viewers, but not contributions,[64] since religion is supposed to come free.

The existence of favored churches also encourages government hindrance and harassment of other churches. The French government has officially designated 173 religious groups (most of them Evangelical Protestants, including Baptists) as dangerous cults, imposing heavy tax burdens upon them and subjecting their members to official discrimination in such things as employment. Subsequently, Belgium has outdone the French, identifying 189 dangerous cults, including the Quakers, the YWCA (but not the YMCA), Hasidic Jews, Assemblies of God, the Amish, Buddhists, and Seventh-day Adventists. But even groups not condemned by parliamentary action are targets of government interference. As the distinguished British sociologist James Beckford noted, all across Europe government bureaucrats impose "administrative sanctions . . . behind a curtain of official detachment."[65] Many Protestant groups report waiting for years to obtain a building permit for a church, or even for a permit to allow an existing building to be used as a church. Such tactics are especially common in Scandinavian nations where it is often ruled that there is "no need" for an additional church in some area, so no permit is granted.[66] In Germany, many Pentecostal groups have been denied tax-free status unless they register with the government as secular groups such as sports clubs rather than as churches. Subsequently the government sometimes revokes their tax-exempt status and imposes unpayable fines and back-tax demands on congregations.[67]

Nevertheless, many European scholars are adamant that their nations enjoy full religious liberty. To challenge that claim, it no longer is necessary to recite examples of state intrusions because Brian Grim and Roger Finke[68] have created quantitative measures of government interference in religious life. They based their coding on the highly respected annual *International Religious Freedom Report* produced by the U.S. State Department. One of Grim and Finke's measures is the Government Favoritism Index, which is based on "subsidies, privileges, support, or favorable sanctions provided by the state to a select religion or a small group of religions." This index varies from 0.0 (no favoritism) to 10.0 (extreme favoritism). The United States and Taiwan score 0.0 and Saudi Arabia and Iran each score 9.3. While Afghanistan and the United Arab Emirates score 7.8, so do Iceland, Spain, and Greece. Belgium scores 7.5, slightly higher than Bangladesh's 7.3 and India's 7.0. Morocco scores 6.3, while Denmark scores 6.7; Finland, 6.5; Austria 6.2; Switzerland 5.8; France, 5.5; Italy, 5.3; and Norway 5.2. Europe clearly has a religious market highly distorted by government policies of favoritism.

"Enlightened" Teachings

Not content to make little or no effort to arouse public religious participation, in much of Europe the dominant churches, especially the Protestant state churches, have modeled themselves on those American denominations that have been declining so precipitously. In the name of theological enlightenment they offer extremely inexpensive religion, stripped of moral demands and of all but the vaguest sort of supernaturalism. Shortly before the American Episcopal bishop John Shelby Spong began to demonstrate that atheism was acceptable to his fellow bishops, in 1963 the English Anglican bishop John A. T. Robinson published *Honest to God*. In it he dismissed the traditional image of God as a conscious being as an unbelievable "caricature," an outdated and immature image of "an old man in the sky." He proceeded to explain Tillich's definition of God so carefully that any reader could grasp that this "God" was nothing more than a vague aspect of human psychology. The book was an instant best-seller in Britain and the next year in the United States, where many mainline leaders promptly hailed it, as many of his fellow English bishops had done. Subsequently, many English churchmen have published books ridiculing the central tenets of Christianity. Countless similar examples can be cited from the continent—especially Scandinavia. More important, these views have gained wide currency among the rank-and-file clergy.

In this regard, the recent case of a parish priest in the Church of Denmark is instructive. Thorkild Grosbøll served for many years as the priest of the Danish Church in Tarbaek, a town about ten miles north of Copenhagen. In 2003 he published a book in which he explained that he did not believe in God. This attracted some attention and led to an interview with a national newspaper in which Grosbøll said, "God belongs in the past. He actually is so old-fashioned that I am baffled by modern people believing in his existence. I am thoroughly fed up with empty words about miracles and eternal life."[69] Subsequently, he told the *New York Times*, "I do not believe in a physical God, in the afterlife, in the resurrection, in the Virgin Mary. . . . And I believe Jesus was [only] a nice guy."[70] Nevertheless, Grosbøll planned to continue as a priest, obviously assuming that his beliefs were within the acceptable limits of the Danish Church, which indeed appears to be the case. After a hearing before an ecclesiastical court, Grosbøll resumed serving as a parish priest after reconfirming his priestly vows, but without recanting any of his views—although he was instructed not to talk to the press.

This was not a freak event. The Scandinavian state churches have been flirting with irreligion for at least a century. Consider that in Sweden the church has been largely controlled locally by elected boards, the candidates being nominated by the national political parties. Hence, for several generations the favored candidates were socialists, which often has resulted in placing avowed atheists in charge of the church. "Members of parish boards and the church council are elected more for their political positions and conviction than for their religious faith. No religious qualifications are required of the candidates—indeed, they need not even be baptized or confirmed. The state church is governed by a majority of nonbelievers—citizens who seldom or never attend church services."[71] As with other Scandinavian state churches, until disestablishment was adopted in 2006, the Church of Sweden was controlled by the Ministry of Ecclesiastical Affairs, and for many years the minister of Ecclesiastical Affairs was Alva Myrdahl, a well-know leftist economist and nonbeliever. She was inspired to appoint a commission to compose a new Swedish translation of the New Testament, on grounds that "the timeworn Holy Bible [is] becoming increasingly marginalized in the modern, rational, world view."[72] Even its ardent supporters acknowledged that this translation (published in 1981) contains "sweeping transformation[s] of accepted interpretations. . . . In important ways, it must of necessity run against the grain of Bible traditions."[73] This demystified translation is now the official Church of Sweden version. Is it really any wonder that by far the majority of the Swedes who are in church on a Sunday attend small Protestant denominations that oppose the state church?

It is also instructive that the Roman Catholic Church has nowhere in Europe been at the mercy of the state via-à-vis its teachings and scriptures. And religion remains far stronger in the Catholic nations of Europe than in the Protestant regions.[74]

Conclusion

Given that America is so much more religious than Europe, if religion does result in many individual and social benefits, then America ought to be substantially better off than Europe in terms of these matters. And it is!

* 2 *

Crime and Prosocial Behavior

M OST MAJOR American universities have a department of criminology, and many scholarly journals are devoted to that subject. Nonetheless, criminology is only half of a field of study. As it stands, criminology is devoted entirely to asking why people do bad things; it never asks why people do good things—why they engage in prosocial rather than antisocial behavior. Obviously, these two aspects of human activity are intimately connected, and social factors influencing one usually influence the other. Hence, antisocial and prosocial behavior are both examined in this chapter.

As we will see, a large body of solid research shows that both anti- and prosocial behaviors, are greatly influenced by religion. An inventory of research studies published between 1944 and 2010 found 247 that reported a positive effect of religion on reducing crime, deviance, and delinquency—often a very strong effect.[1] Amazingly, a very recent examination of sixteen popular criminology textbooks revealed that fourteen did not have the word "religion" (or any variant thereof) in their index, while another had the word "religiosity" in its index, but devoted only one brief paragraph to its effect on crime. The sixteenth book devoted two pages to answering the question "Does Religion Reduce Delinquency?" and erroneously concluded that it has only a very trivial effect.[2] For textbook authors to have ignored such a massive research literature reflects not only their own biases but also their awareness of the unwavering antireligion prejudice of so many university faculty who might adopt their book. Indeed, the lengthy article on "crime" in Wikipedia devotes only four sentences to "Religion and Crime," and these are entirely limited to noting that some activities have been "criminalized on religious grounds," citing "alcohol consumption . . . abortion and stem-cell research." The accompanying picture shows an anti-Jewish riot in Germany in 1819, above the caption reading, "Religious sentiment often becomes a contributory factor of crime." Not a word even hints that religion may keep anyone on the straight and narrow.

Still, a major question arises: If religiousness reduces crime, and since America is an unusually religious nation, why are our crime rates so much higher than those of far less religious nations, such as those of Western Europe?

They aren't.

CRIME-RIDDEN AMERICA?

The image of the United States as a crime-ridden society has several bases. It no doubt began when ours was a frontier society culminating in the era of the Wild West—stories of western gunfighters were as popular in Europe as in the settled areas of America. This image of American crime and violence probably was further encouraged by the mob wars of the Prohibition era. In addition, the American homicide rate is indeed substantially higher than the rates in Western Europe, although our rate is much lower than in some parts of Eastern Europe (the Russian homicide rate is more than twice as high as ours) and the rates in Latin America are many times higher. But a major basis for the misconceptions about crime in the United States is that for many years ours were the only published official crime statistics.

Since the early 1930s, under the supervision of the Federal Bureau of Investigation (FBI), each year every American law enforcement agency has reported all crimes reported to them, organized by offense categories. These data are then tabulated and published, broken down in a number of useful ways, in a volume known as the *Uniform Crime Report*. So, for decades, Europeans had statistical proof that America is wicked and violent. When European nations finally began to gather and publish their own statistics no one paid much attention, even though their rates tend to be far higher than ours. I believe that I was the first social science textbook author to include some comparisons between American and European crime rates,[3] and very few have followed my example. Incredibly, in 2006 the International Police Organization (Interpol) voted to cease publishing its compendium of national crime statistics and proceeded to withdraw all of its previous reports from its website— presumably such comparisons are not good for the public to know.

In any event, Table 2.1 reports the most recent national crime statistics I was able to locate in order to demonstrate that, compared with much of Western Europe, America has low crime rates.

Denmark has nearly two-and-a-half times as many burglaries per 100,000 population as does the United States, while the U.S. rate also is exceeded by Austria, Switzerland, the United Kingdom, Sweden, Belgium, and the Netherlands. Comparing theft rates, the table shows that Sweden has a rate twice as high as that of the United States and that Denmark, the United Kingdom, Norway, Germany, and Finland also have higher theft rates. As for "violent America," the assault rate in Sweden is about three-and-a-half times that of the United States, and the rates also are far higher in the United Kingdom, Belgium, Finland, Germany, Ireland, the Netherlands, Portugal, and France.

Of course, the American homicide rate remains higher than those for Western European nations. In 2008 the U.S. rate was 5.1 per 100,000 population, compared with 2.5 in Finland, 2.2

TABLE 2.1. COMPARING AMERICAN AND WESTERN EUROPEAN CRIME RATES (2008)

Burglaries per 100,000 Population	
Denmark	1,715.0
Austria	1,203.3
Switzerland	1,146.8
United Kingdom	1,068.2
Sweden	1,024.3
Belgium	848.8
Netherlands	738.4
United States	713.0

Thefts Per 100,000 Population	
Sweden	4,255.8
Denmark	3,482.8
United Kingdom	3,012.6
Norway	2,647.2
Germany	2,399.1
Finland	2,266.3
United States	2,114.1

Assaults Per 100,000 Population	
Sweden	918.7
United Kingdom	769.8
Belgium	696.6
Finland	655.6
Germany	630.3
Ireland	388.6
Netherlands	361.3
Portugal	313.7
France	303.2
United States	267.9

Source: United Nations Office on Drugs and Crime 2009.

in Scotland, 2.0 in Ireland, 1.8 in Belgium, 1.4 in Denmark and France, 1.2 in Italy, and 0.5 in Austria. Here, two factors must be considered. First, European nations report high *attempted* murder rates. But, unlike in America where approximately 80 percent of all homicides are committed with firearms, few in Europe possess guns and hence most of their attempts at murder fail. The second factor is race. The American homicide rate (for 2007) based on only white victims (3.1) is far closer to the Western European rates; African Americans (20.9) are about seven times as likely to be murdered.[4] Many efforts have been made to explain interracial differences in homicide rates, none of them very convincing. Moreover, efforts to explain African American homicide rates probably should be extended to explain the very high rates in Eastern Europe and Latin America. Consider that the homicide rate is 14.2 in Russia, 21.5 in the Dominican Republic, 38.8 in Colombia, and 59.5 in Jamaica.

Any effort even to summarize the literature on the causes of African American crime rates would take a volume by itself. Here the important point remains that religion exerts its suppressive effects on crime among African Americans as well as among other Americans. And it is religious effects that help explain the lower American crime rates shown in Table 2.1.

RELIGION AND CRIME

Crime consists of violations of the law by adults; when minors commit the same actions, it's called "delinquency." One of the most remarkable facts about criminological research is that it has been focused almost exclusively on delinquency. Of the 247 studies mentioned earlier dealing with religion and behavior, I could only discover two based on adults and devoted to crime, as opposed to other forms of deviance such as alcohol abuse or domestic violence, and both studies were limited to small samples, each drawn from one city.[5] One reason for the focus on teenagers seems to be the notion that delinquency is the primary crime problem—that by the time offenders reach adulthood it is too late to reform them. The more likely reason is cost and convenience. Almost all studies of delinquency are based on high school students—usually from a single community. Even the few national studies are based on stratified samples in which a random sample of schools is selected, and then either all of the students within these schools are studied, or a sample of them. Then, nearly without exception, the data are collected by use of questionnaires filled out by each student during school hours. Sometimes school records are added to each student's data file, and once in a while, parents fill out a questionnaire also, but the focus is on matters involving their child, not their own behavior vis-à-vis the law. To base studies on questionnaires administered in class at one or a few locations is quite inexpensive; studies based on interviews with national samples are very expensive.

The only good nationwide data on adult offending of which I am aware were collected in several of the General Social Surveys (GSS) conducted annually since 1972 and based on national samples of adults. The purpose of the GSS is to make data on a variety of issues freely available to all interested researchers. In five of its early surveys, the GSS included a self-report item on crime. As far as I know, I am the only person who ever made any use of these data.[6] Some have suggested that these GSS data were not used because they are self-reports and hence untrustworthy. But virtually *all* studies of delinquency are based on self-report data, and these have turned out to be surprisingly reliable when compared with official police records.[7] I suspect that the GSS data went unused because sociologists and political scientists have run the study, and the social sciences have become so specialized that criminologists who might have been interested never became aware of them. (I questioned several prominent criminologists who said they had never heard of these GSS data.)

In any event,Tables 2.2A and B report my findings from these five national surveys. Results from each survey were so similar that merging all five years was appropriate. Hence, the results shown here are extremely reliable, being based on more than nine thousand cases.

TABLE 2.2A. PERCENTAGE OF ADULTS WHO REPORT HAVING BEEN PICKED UP BY THE POLICE

Denomination	Number of Cases	Percent Picked Up
Protestant	6,081	10%
Catholic	2,590	11%
Jewish	236	5%
None	714	25%
All	9,621	11%

Each respondent was asked, "Were you ever picked up, or charged, by the police for any reason whether or not you were guilty?" Eleven percent agreed that they had been picked up. Since respondents were not asked *when* this happened, some of these incidents probably occurred while they still were juveniles. Moreover, many people no doubt got away with an offense or two without having been picked up. However, based on arrest statistics, there is little reason to think that the estimate that one in ten Americans has been picked up by the police is far from reality.[8]

In any event, the data strongly support the claim that religion deters crime. As for religious denominations, Jews (5 percent) are the least likely to have been picked up by the police, and those without a religion (25 percent) are by far the most likely to have been picked up. As for church attendance, those who never attend are about four times as likely to have been picked up as

those who attend weekly. As is well known, men are more likely
than women to get in trouble with the law, but the church attendance effect is strong for both sexes. Similarly, African Americans are more likely than whites to have been picked up, but
within both races the weekly church attenders are far less likely
to have been picked up than are those who never go to church.
In addition, (not shown in Table 2.2) the religious effect remains
very strong within levels of education and income. Finally, the
effects of religion hold in every major region of the country.
Notice, however, that people in the West are more likely to have
been picked up. These two findings about region become significant in the next section on delinquency.

TABLE 2.2B. PERCENTAGE OF ADULTS WHO REPORT HAVING
BEEN PICKED UP BY THE POLICE

Church Attendance	All	Women	Men	White	African American
Weekly	6%	3%	10%	5%	10%
Sometimes	13%	5%	21%	12%	18%
Never	21%	9%	32%	20%	30%

Church Attendance	East	Midwest	South	West
Weekly	5%	6%	5%	8%
Sometimes	11%	13%	13%	15%
Never	18%	18%	19%	27%

Source: Computed by the author from General Social Surveys 1973; 1974; 1976; 1977; 1980;
1982; 1984.

If adult crime has been ignored, adult drug use has not. For
example, in 2002 the General Social Survey asked, "Have you
ever, even once, used 'crack' cocaine in chunk or rock form?"
In response, 4.8 percent of Americans said, "Yes." Broken down

by church attendance, 2.7 percent of weekly attenders admitted using crack, compared with 7.2 percent of those who never attend—a difference that is highly statistically significant. The same survey also asked, "Have you ever, even once, taken any drug by injection with a needle—do not include anything you took under doctor's orders?" To this, 2.5 percent of Americans said, "Yes." Only 1.5 percent of weekly attenders answered affirmatively, compared with 4.9 percent of nonattenders; this, too, is highly significant.

Religion and Delinquency

The discovery that religion decreases the tendency of minors to break the law is a convoluted tale in which I played a leading and misleading role. Early in my career, when I was a research sociologist on the staff of the Survey Research Center at the University of California–Berkeley, one of my colleagues and close friends was Travis Hirschi. While I was busy writing books on the sociology of religion, he conducted an innovative study of delinquent behavior based on a sample of teenagers in Richmond, California. Then Hirschi wrote up his findings in *Causes of Delinquency*,[9] a book that has since become a classic.

After Hirschi had submitted the book to a publisher I happened to be one of the sociologists selected to read the manuscript and advise the publisher whether to publish it. Of course, I told them, "Yes." Then one day at lunch, Hirschi and I got into a casual discussion of the book, and I happened to mention that it contained not a word about the effects of religion. I knew that he had collected data on the religious beliefs and church participation of the teenagers in his sample. Hirschi replied that he could find no religious effects on delinquency. I was very surprised, recognizing immediately that such a finding was big news. A quick search of the literature revealed no prior research on the subject, so we wrote a paper, "Hellfire and Delinquency," to report our finding that kids who attended church regularly and believed in hell were as likely as irreligious kids to steal, vandalize, and commit other delinquent acts.

Probably because it was so supportive of the antireligious biases of academia, the paper was accepted immediately and quickly published in a leading journal.[10] Several years later a second study, based on high school students in Oregon, reported the same thing we had: no religious effects on delinquency.[11] But then came two studies, one based on students in Atlanta and one on students in Utah, both of which found what everyone would have expected to find: a strong negative correlation between church attendance and delinquency.[12] So, now what? Does religion suppress delinquency or not?

It took a long time for the light to dawn. In other work on the geography of American religion I discovered an "unchurched belt" running along the Pacific Coast. In 1970, about 60 percent of Americans belonged to a local church congregation, but in Washington and Oregon only 33 percent belonged; in California, 36 percent; in Alaska, 37 percent; in Hawaii, 38 percent; and in Nevada, 39 percent.[13] Since then membership has risen everywhere, but still it lags in these states—except for California, where the membership rate has risen considerably. One day I noticed that the two studies finding no religion effects were conducted in this unchurched belt, while the two studies finding religious effects were in places with high church-membership rates. Perhaps *religious effects are muffled by an unchurched majority*. To test this notion I gained access to an excellent new delinquency study based on students in Seattle. If I was right, there should have been no religious effects on delinquency in this sample. And there were none.[14]

Years later I was able to greatly increase the certainty that religious contexts explained the variations in the findings. Gaining access to a national sample including 11,995 teenagers, I examined the relationship between religion and delinquency in *each* of the five main census regions of the nation. In four of them—the East, Midwest, South, and Mountain regions—religiousness had a strong, negative effect on delinquency.[15] But in the Pacific region, home of the unchurched belt, there was no religious effect. Welcome to the *moral community*.

MORAL COMMUNITIES

Life is social. It is through day-to-day interaction with others that we embrace moral standards, including what qualify as "immoral" standards. If our friends think it is wrong to steal, we probably think so, too. If they think it okay to steal as long as you don't get caught, that may become our view as well. Religious considerations may or may not enter into what moral standards we adopt. If most of our friends are religious, then religious standards probably enter into our moral outlook. But if most of our friends are not religious, then religious considerations tend not to enter into the process by which our moral standards are formulated and adopted. For, even if we are religious, even if we bring up religious concerns vis-à-vis moral matters, these would not strike a responsive chord with most of our associates. In this way, the effect of individual religious commitment is smothered by group irreligiousness and tends to become a compartmentalized component of the lives of the religious. This is facilitated because, as studies show, among students attending public schools (as most do) there is little tendency for those with conventional religious commitments to give them weight in selecting friends. That is, with the exception of kids in religious schools, or with intense religious backgrounds, religion plays little or no role in shaping interpersonal attachments. Therefore, in relatively unchurched communities (as in the unchurched belt), the religious kids tend to have mainly unchurched associates.[14] Of course, the opposite occurs in communities where most people are religious. When most people in a friendship network are religious, religious concerns are amplified and made a valid consideration when future actions are being considered. In such communities, individual variations in teenage religiousness come into play simply because *individual commitment is energized by the group*.

In moral communities as defined here, the majority of people are religious and religious standards inform morality. Based on the percentages of their populations who currently belong to a church, Reno (28 percent), Seattle (36 percent), and Portland, Oregon (37 percent), are not moral communities, while Omaha (60 percent), Memphis (69 percent), and Philadelphia (71 percent) are.[17] We would expect religiousness to be strongly related to delinquency in the latter three cities, but not in the first three.

Recall, however, that a strong religious effect held among *adults* in the western region; this muffling effect thus appears to *only affect teenagers*. The reason is that adults do tend to select their friends on the basis of their religiousness. Studies show that more religious adults, and especially those in more conservative denominations, tend to select most or all of their best friends from their church congregations.[18] Hence, even in a city such as Reno, religious effects among adults are often amplified by reinforcement from one's friends. In addition, a very creative study by Mark Regnerus of the University of Texas found that high schools can function effectively as moral communities and that the effect is not simply on/off but a matter of degree: the greater the proportion of religious students in a school, the stronger the effect of religion on delinquency at the individual level.[19]

However, quite aside from the influence of the moral community upon the effects of individual religiousness are the direct effects of the moral community on crime. Just as we have seen that the overall higher degree of religiousness of the United States relative to the nations of Western Europe is matched by American crime rates being lower than those of many European nations, so, too, the more religious American communities also ought to have lower crime rates than do the less religious communities, and they do. Recall from Table 2.2 that residents of the West, at all three levels of church attendance, were more likely than people elsewhere to have been picked up by the police. This is consistent with lower church attendance and membership rates in this same area, and with official crime statistics that show higher rates in the Western states and cities.

Based on the nation's major cities, the following generalizations not only are supported by recent data, but also by data going as far back as the 1920s.[20]

- ► The higher a city's church membership rate, the lower its burglary rate.
- ► The higher a city's church membership rate, the lower its larceny rate.
- ► The higher a city's church membership rate, the lower its robbery rate.
- ► The higher a city's church membership rate, the lower its assault rate.
- ► The higher a city's church membership rate, the lower its homicide rate.

However, the church membership rate is less strongly related to the assault and homicide rates than to the other crime rates— probably because many assaults and homicides are crimes of passion in which the offender acted on impulse and gave little or no thought to moral concerns.[21]

RECIDIVISM AND PRISON MINISTRIES

Few people today realize that prisons, as places where people serve sentences for crimes, are quite new. For centuries prisons and jails were merely places where people were held while awaiting trial or until they received their sentences. Punishment did not involve spending time in prison but instead took the form of execution, mutilation, torture, branding, flogging, or enslavement. Not until the late eighteenth century was confinement used as an alternative to physical punishment.

The initial use of confinement began in Pennsylvania under the direction of William Penn (1644–1718), whose Quaker beliefs caused him to oppose physical punishment. Penn directed that those convicted of crimes spend a sentence at hard labor to pay for their own upkeep and to refund damages to their victims. But his prisons soon became notorious for vice, so in 1790 the Quakers of Pennsylvania tried a new approach: the penitentiary.

This new name reflected that this institution was to be a place where offenders were forced to contemplate their sins and become penitent. Hence, each prisoner was placed in an isolated eight-foot-by-eight-foot cell and forced to live in silence. But it didn't work. Those released after completing their sentences seldom were reformed; they committed new offenses. Then came the modern "therapeutic" prison. Convinced by social scientists, especially psychologists, that what was needed to reform offenders was therapeutic counseling through which they could gain the insights needed to help them go straight, the federal and state governments devoted huge sums to staffing prisons with therapists and social workers. These efforts were pursued for nearly a century, until overburdened by excessive costs. Throughout, the *recidivism rate* (the percentage of offenders who are rearrested and resentenced) has remained steady at about 70 percent. That is, the great majority of those in jails and prisons have been there before and, if released, will soon be back again. In the past few decades, various religious groups have made substantial efforts to help reduce recidivism.

Everyone who has ever been around prisons knows about jailhouse conversions—inmates who become deeply religious, sincerely regret their wicked past, and go on to lead exemplary lives. This was, of course, what Penn had hoped would happen in his penitentiaries, and these examples have continued to inspire religious efforts at prisoner reform. During the past twenty years or so, the involvement of religious Americans in prison ministries has become a very large undertaking. Literally tens of thousands of volunteers are involved in such programs, the most well-known being Chuck Colson's Prison Fellowship, which currently has about fifty thousand volunteers. These prison ministries do not merely meet with, proselytize, and counsel offenders while they are in prison, but continue to offer them guidance and group encouragement after their release.

But do these programs work? A well-done study has reported that participation in a prison ministry program significantly reduced antisocial behavior of prisoners while they were still in prison.[22] But what about recidivism? Everyone involved believes that prison ministry programs do reduce recidivism, but it is impossible to conduct research that can adequately demonstrate whether they really do. The proper way to assess any such program would be to select a large group of prisoners who are within several years of discharge and randomly assign half of them to take part in a prison ministry program. Then, after they have been released, compare the recidivism of those assigned to the program with those who were not. Because random assignment rules out initial differences between the two groups, this subsequent comparison would provide strong evidence on whether the program worked, and if so, to what degree.

Unfortunately, it would be illegal to assign prisoners to a religious program. Consequently, all studies must contrast those who volunteered to participate in a prison ministry program with those who did not. There are compelling reasons to assume that the volunteers are different from nonvolunteers—for example, that volunteers are overrecruited from those who are less likely to return to crime in any event. Consequently, the comparisons that show that participants do in fact have a substantially lower recidivism rate[23] cannot demonstrate that the programs are effective, although a lack of differences would offer strong evidence that the programs do not work. I would hazard the guess that the programs do have a positive effect, if for no other reason than that they continue to offer a supportive network to participants after they have been released. But the matter cannot be settled. It should be acknowledged that leaders of these ministries are quite realistic about assessing and improving their programs. This is especially important because all reform efforts must be based on volunteers since it is out of the question to match their efforts with paid professionals. And only the religious community is able to enlist the needed legions of volunteers.

Prosocial Behavior

Many of the most significant forms of prosocial behavior are considered in later chapters—such as being a generous donor and a ready volunteer, being a good parent and a faithful spouse. In contrast, the examples of prosocial behavior taken up below may seem rather inconsequential. One reason is that almost no intentional studies of prosocial behavior have taken place; no university departments specialize in the subject, no journals are devoted to the topic, and no research grants reward interest in such matters. Moreover, very few of those who have studied any form of prosocial behavior have had any interest in religious effects. Hence, an immense review of the research literature on altruism does not even include the words "religion" or "religiousness."[24] Another reason for the neglect of prosocial behavior is that good deeds don't seem to have as much impact as bad deeds; donating a kidney seems to pale in comparison with stabbing someone to death, just as helping an elderly woman carry her groceries home is not nearly as significant as snatching her purse. On the other hand, prosocial behavior makes social life not only tolerable but even possible.

Honesty

A number of studies have assessed the importance of religiousness for honesty in various contexts. Robin Perrin presented all students in one of his classes at Pepperdine University with their returned examinations, each of which had been incorrectly scored, awarding each student an extra point. Then he presented the students with the correct answers and asked each to notify him whether their exam had been correctly graded, had incorrectly given them an extra point, or incorrectly had given them a point too little. A third of the students honestly reported they had incorrectly been given an extra point. Two-thirds claimed they were owed a point, or that their exam had been correctly graded—knowing full well that they really had been given an extra point. Since earlier in the term, each student had filled out a questionnaire including measures of religiousness, it was possible to compare the honesty of students separated by religiousness. Results: 45 percent of the weekly attenders were honest, compared with 13 percent of those who never or rarely attended church.[25]

A somewhat similar study gave students in business administration an opportunity to increase their chances of winning money by falsely reporting their performance on a word-search puzzle. Unbeknownst to the students, their true performances could be recovered. Student religiousness was the strongest factor predicting honest reporting.[26]

"Niceness"

A surprising number of good studies are devoted to this question: Are religious people nice people? The earlier studies used self-reported items to measure "niceness." Several of these items were:

True or False

"I have never intensely disliked anyone."

"When I see a child crying, I usually stop and comfort him."

Of course, respondents could easily lie, and no doubt some
did. But the fact remains that when these items were posed to a
national sample of Americans, irreligious people were far more
likely than religious people to say "false."[37]

In 2002 the General Social Survey asked a national sample
of Americans whether during the past year they had allowed
someone to go ahead of them in a checkout line. Twenty-one
percent of those who attended church said they had not done
so, compared with 12 percent of the nonattenders.

Later studies have had the advantage of a far more objec-
tive measure of niceness. When surveys are based on personal
interviews, it is possible to have the interviewer code various
things about the person being interviewed, such as baldness,
obesity, or the respondent's attitude during the interview. The
National Opinion Research Center often does the latter, providing these categories: (1) friendly and interested; (2) cooperative, but not particularly interested; (3) impatient and restless;
and (4) hostile. A recent study[28] used this as a four-point scale
measuring "niceness." Three measures of religiousness were
used: frequency of church attendance, frequency of prayer, and
self-reported degree of religiousness. After extensive statistical
analysis, all three measures of religion were found to be highly
related to perceived niceness.

Blood Donors

In 2002 the General Social Survey asked a national sample
of Americans whether during the past year they had donated
blood. Twenty percent of weekly church attenders said they had
done so, compared with 9 percent of the nonattenders.

Additional research studies have found that

▸ Religious Americans are more likely to wear their seatbelts and much less likely to drink and drive.[29]
▸ Religious Americans are more likely to stand during the playing of the National Anthem.[30]
▸ Religious Americans are more likely to use trash bins rather than to litter.[31]
▸ Religious American teenagers are more likely to attend school regularly (rather than be truants).[32]

CONCLUSION

All Americans are safer and their property more secure because this is such a religious nation. The average person in "irreligious" Sweden is three-and-a-half times as likely as the average American to be criminally assaulted, and twice as likely to be the victim of theft. Religious Americans are far less likely than the irreligious to commit crimes and far more likely to commit prosocial actions. Consequently, the higher the church membership of a city, the lower its crime rates. Even ignoring the immense amount of personal suffering and financial loss that Americans are spared because of this religious blessing, as is seen in this book's final chapter, America's religiousness results in huge amounts of governmental savings.

* 3 *

Fertility and Family

EUROPE IS DISAPPEARING. Not just Western Europe, but the whole continent.

Of course, the land mass will remain; it is the people who are disappearing, taking with them the culture that has defined "Europe" for several millennia.[1] The cause of it all is the demise of the European family and especially the erosion of one of its primary features: *fertility*. Even assuming that the birth rates of European nations do not continue to decline, they already are so far below replacement level that, unless dramatic changes occur, there will be no Germans left in Germany, no Swedes in Sweden, no Poles in Poland—no Europeans anywhere in Europe—in less than two centuries. Meanwhile, increasingly smaller younger generations will stagger under the burden of supporting larger populations of elderly. Soon in many nations there will be fewer than one working person to support each retired person.

This catastrophe is not happening in the United States. The American fertility rate is slightly above replacement level and is rising. And the reason for the American exception is religion. The fertility of churchgoing Europeans is well above replacement level, but churchgoing Europeans are too few to offset the infertility of the less religious and the irreligious. In America, the higher fertility of the religious majority makes up for the low fertility of others. Thus, one of the primary blessings of

American faith is that we are not faced with the many problems resulting from a shrinking population. Additionally, Americans enjoy many other benefits from having a higher percentage of happily married couples who not only beget more children, but do a superior job of child rearing. These aspects of family life also are highly related to religiousness.

THE DEPOPULATION BOMB

The total fertility rate (TFR) is the number of children born to the average female during her lifetime. Under modern conditions the TFR needed to keep a population from declining in size is about 2.05 per female—one child to replace the mother, one to replace the father, and an occasional child to offset infant mortality. The current American TFR is 2.10 and slowly rising. In contrast, every nation in Europe has a TFR below replacement level, most of them well below (Italy's TFR is 1.41, and Poland's is 1.39), and in all of these nations the TFR continues to decline. Low fertility partly results from the use of contraception, but also by the widespread use of abortion to terminate pregnancies—about one-fourth of all Swedish pregnancies are aborted, as are about 45 percent in Russia. Of course, the reason for low fertility is that fewer people want children, and those who do want fewer than their parents did.

Amazingly, many prominent observers do not worry about depopulation, but continue to be concerned about the so-called Population Bomb. During the 1960s and early 1970s there was an incredible panic generated by the above-replacement birth rates that occurred in many Western nations during the baby boom in the aftermath of World War II and by the rapid population growth in the developing nations as progress in public health had greatly reduced their death rates. The most dire consequences were taken for granted. Stanford University biologist Paul Ehrlich's best-seller, *The Population Bomb* (1968), began,

"The battle to feed all of humanity is over. In the 1970s the world will undergo famines—hundreds of millions are going to starve to death." In 1974 the famous British novelist and scientist C. P. Snow told the *New York Times*, "Perhaps in ten years millions of people in the poor countries are going to starve to death before our very eyes. . . . We shall see them doing so on our television sets."[2]

Of course, nothing of the sort happened. The food supply increased far more rapidly than did the population. Even in the "hopelessly backward" less-developed nations, when reduced infant mortality no longer required families to have many children, birth rates soon dropped rapidly, and the population bomb turned into a dud. Meanwhile, the baby boom in the industrialized nations proved to be very brief, and fertility rates returned to the long-term trend toward depopulation that had dominated social science textbooks prior to World War II. In her influential book *The Menace of Underpopulation* (1936), Enid Charles, the Canadian demographer, wrote that in Western Europe "the population has already ceased to be capable of maintaining its numbers."

Nevertheless, fear of the population bomb remains an article of faith in many intellectual circles, prompting many prominent Europeans (and Americans) to welcome depopulation. Having carefully reported the impending depopulation of Europe—noting, for example, that Italy's population will shrink from 57.2 million to "no more than 45 million people in 2050"—Oxford's prominent environmentalist Norman Myers stresses the "highly positive point to all this." In an essay in *Population Press*, Myers asserted that "fewer people in Europe . . . will mean less pressure on natural resources of all kinds" and will certainly help prevent "global warming." He went on to approvingly include the above-cited Paul Ehrlich as one of many "experts" who are urging that "Europe and America should consider a long term commitment to cutting back on its human numbers in light of its drain on planetary resources."[3] In another essay published several months later, Myers condemned all who are concerned about population decline, claiming that "we are [still] living in the biggest population explosion in human history,"[4] despite the fact that birth rates are rapidly declining in most nations on earth. Even in the Islamic nations, the TFR is falling so rapidly that most will soon be below the replacement level; Iran's is now only 1.78.

Why do so many intellectuals still cling to the threat of the population bomb? Anxiety about the fact that America is still growing is at least partly to blame. For anti-Americanism has replaced anti-Semitism as the common currency of European intellectualism—Myers condemns America as "the most over-populated of all countries."[5] Anti-Christianity also plays a major role. Myers no doubt agrees with his colleague Ward McAfee, who wrote in the same journal that Christianity is to blame for America's continued fertility, adding that "Christianity (which continues to contribute to the earth crisis) is in need of some serious pruning" in order to become "less human-centered."[6] These views reflect hopes for restoring the earth to some semblance of prehistoric times when the human population has been reduced to tiny bands living close to the earth, as so often reflected in radical Green proposals, such as allowing all the farmland of the Great Plains states to return to wilderness. For those of us who do not identify with television survival shows, such a transformation would be tragic.

It also seems unlikely. Humans are not puppets. We are not condemned to march to the beat of historical inevitability. And just as human self-interest led to the disarming of the population bomb, a shift in prevailing human values may halt the trend toward depopulation—a matter that is assessed below.

Of course, McAfee is correct to link fertility to religion. Besides America, the only Western nations with a TFR above replacement level are Ireland (2.07) and Israel (2.96).

RELIGION AND FERTILITY

Today, the primary factor in fertility is whether people want many or few children. In 1994 the International Social Survey Project asked national samples in various European nations, "All in all, what do you think is the ideal number of children for a family to have?" The results are shown in Table 3.1.

TABLE 3.1. PERCENTAGE WHO THINK THE IDEAL NUMBER OF CHILDREN IS THREE OR MORE

Church or Synagogue Attendance	Weekly	Sometimes	Never	Total
Israel	89%	88%	75%	83%
Ireland	74%	55%	43%	68%
Norway	71%	57%	39%	51%
Poland	51%	40%	28%	44%
Netherlands	69%	47%	32%	43%
Slovenia	68%	33%	26%	36%
Sweden	61%	36%	31%	35%
Italy	37%	24%	20%	28%
Germany*	42%	23%	19%	25%
Austria	45%	21%	12%	24%
United Kingdom	37%	25%	18%	23%
Bulgaria	31%	23%	19%	22%
Czech Republic	40%	23%	17%	21%

*West Germany only

Source: International Social Survey Program 1994.

Prior research has shown that people tend to give an ideal number that is greater than the number that most of them end up having. Even so, only small minorities in most of Europe responded with the number three or higher. Only in Ireland and Israel (and barely in Norway) did a majority favor more than two children. But in every nation, the percentage favoring a family of three or more children was strongly related to church attendance.

As these findings indicate, Europe's lack of fertility is directly attributable to its lack of religiousness. Table 3.2 was assembled by Tomas Frejka of the Max Planck Institute in Germany and Charles F. Westoff of Princeton University.[7] They merged many samples in order to accumulate a very large number of cases. The results are definitive.

TABLE 3.2. AVERAGE NUMBER OF CHILDREN BORN
TO WOMEN AGES 35–44

Church Attendance	United States	Europe
More than weekly	2.34	2.74
Weekly	2.17	2.23
1–3 times a month	2.12	1.93
Less than once a month	1.86	1.83
Never	1.70	1.79

Source: Frejka and Westoff 2008.

In both Europe and America, fertility is highly related to church attendance. In fact, among those who attend church more often than weekly, European women have a higher fertility rate than do Americans, and both European and American women who attend weekly have a fertility rate well above replacement level—as do American women who attend only several times a month. The trouble is that while nearly 40 percent of American women attend church at least weekly,[8] a much smaller fraction of European women attend that often (see Table 1.4). And while only about 13 percent of American women rarely or never attend, the majority of European women are nonattenders.

However, the fact that European women who attend church have a well-above-replacement-level fertility rate has an implication that had been missed until the brilliant new work by Eric Kaufmann of the University of London. In his book *Shall the Religious Inherit the Earth?* (2010), Kaufmann noted that only the irreligious sector of Europe's population is declining, while the religious sector is growing. Consequently, rather than Europe's population disappearing, only the irreligious European population may disappear with the result that differential fertility may produce a huge religious revival in Europe. For the continent as a whole, my calculations show the religious population will outnumber the irreligious population in about four more generations! The time span will differ from country to country depending on the current ratio of religious to irreligious, but the eventual outcome will be the same if everything else remains constant. Then, if the birthrate of religious Europeans is sustained at above the replacement level, the population will grow and the churches will be full.

Many social scientists have studied the effect of religion on fertility, but Kaufmann is among the first to note the effect of fertility on religion. Perhaps the first to do so were two Americans[9] who responded to an extensive literature on the "vanishing" American Jew by pointing out that at current fertility levels, while Conservative Jews (TFR = 1.74), Reform Jews (TFR = 1.36), and secular Jews (TFR = 1.29) might soon vanish, they would be far more than replaced by Hasidic Jews (TFR = 6.72) and Orthodox Jews (TFR = 3.39). This replacement would be accelerated by the fact that although intermarriage is rare among the Hasidic and the Orthodox (about 6 percent), intermarriage is very common among Conservative Jews (32 percent), and nearly half of Reform Jews (46 percent) and secular Jews (49 percent) marry non-Jews. As an illustration of what these trends imply, the scholars assumed five groups of Jews, each having 100 members in the first generation. At current fertility and intermarriage rates, by the fourth generation the group of 100 Hasidic Jews would number 3,401, and the Orthodox Jews would number 434; there would be 29 Conservative Jews and 10 Reform Jews; and the group of 100 secular Jews would now number 7.

It might also be the case that the percentage of atheists in the United States has remained constant at about 4 percent for many decades because, given their very low fertility rate, many new atheists must be recruited in each generation in order for the group to not shrink in number. In addition, the children of atheists tend to adopt a religion.[10]

The bottom line is that the admonition to "be fruitful and multiply" still has profound implications for the future of the total population and for the percentage of religious people in Europe and the United States.

RELIGIOUS COUPLES

All the facts testify to the conclusion that the more religious the couple, the more stable, satisfying, and beneficial is their family life. They are more apt to get married, to stay married, and to highly rate their marital satisfaction. As the next chapter shows, they even have more active and gratifying sex lives.

Marriage

Religious Americans are far more likely to marry and to stay married than are the irreligious. Reading across, Table 3.3 shows that among adults ages 30 to 45—the prime marriage years[11]—people who never attend church are twice as likely as the weekly attenders to have never married or to currently be divorced or separated.

TABLE 3.3. MARITAL STATUS OF AMERICANS AGES 30–45
AND CHURCH ATTENDANCE

Marital Status	Church Attendance		
	Weekly	Sometimes	Never
Never married	12%	18%	23%
Divorced/Separated	14%	21%	28%
Married	73%	60%	48%
Widowed	1%	1%	1%
Total	100%	100%	100%

Source: General Social Surveys, combined years.

This religious effect on marriage is reflected in the fact that the American marriage rate (9.8 marriages per year, per 1,000 population) is double that of many European nations; the rate for Sweden is 4.7, and 4.5 for Spain. In part this is due to the fact that in most of Europe, couples are far more apt to live together without getting married than are Americans (7 percent of Americans compared with 16 percent in France and 18 percent in Sweden). But even counting unmarried couples, Americans are more likely to enter into household unions than are Europeans, that being part of the reason for the substantial differences in fertility.

Marital Relations

Here we encounter a militant antireligious bias. Some researchers claim that religious Americans' more traditional views of sex roles leads to justification of religious husbands' mistreatment of their wives. A well-known sociologist has been making these charges at academic meetings for more than twenty years, oblivious to an immense body of well-done research that contradicts her. Not only is there no support for claims that religious husbands, especially those of the Evangelical Protestant variety, are more likely to abuse their wives, there is solid evidence that they are better, more loving husbands.[12] A very strong religion effect persists even after controls for alcohol and substance abuse.[13] That is, religious men are not less likely to abuse their wives only because they are far less likely to be under the influence of liquor or drugs, but because of religious influences per se. Were it otherwise, one would expect Table 3.4 to look very different.

TABLE 3.4. PERCENTAGE WHO SAY THEIR CURRENT MARRIAGE IS VERY HAPPY

Church Attendance	All	White	African American
Weekly	67%	69%	60%
Sometimes	52%	61%	42%
Never	58%	60%	41%

Source: General Social Surveys, combined years.

Reading down the table, although most Americans rate their marriage as very happy, weekly church attenders are more likely to do so than are those who only attend sometimes or who never attend (the differences are statistically significant <.01). The relationship is the same among whites and African Americans, but at all levels of church attendance, whites are substantially more likely to rate their marriages as very happy.

Divorce

Table 3.3 has already revealed that weekly church attenders are only half as likely as those who never attend to currently be divorced. But, of course, many who are married have also been divorced. The International Social Survey Project asked a national sample of Americans as well as samples in various European nations, "Have you ever been divorced?"

Much has been made of the fact that, as shown in Table 3.5, divorce is far more frequent in the United States (about a third have been divorced) than in Western European nations. What has been ignored is that in order for there to be a divorce, there must first be a marriage. Europe's lack of divorces is mainly a function of its lack of marriages (when cohabiters break up, there is no divorce). More significantly in all these nations, church attendance is strongly, negatively related to divorce.

TABLE 3.5. PERCENTAGE WHO HAVE BEEN DIVORCED

	Church Attendance			
	Weekly	Sometimes	Never	Total
United States	25%	34%	45%	33%*
Sweden	9%	20%	26%	21%
Netherlands	6%	13%	20%	15%
Norway	5%	13%	20%	15%
Austria	2%	12%	27%	13%
Germany**	5%	11%	26%	13%
Austria	2%	12%	27%	13%

*31% in the 2008 General Social Survey.
**West Germany only.
Source: International Social Survey Project 1994.

There are probably many reasons that actively religious people enjoy a lower divorce rate. For one thing, they probably place a higher value on marriage and take marriage vows more seriously than low- or nonattenders. Marriage is, after all, held to be a sacred ceremony in many churches and involves consecrated pledges. Religious couples also come into marriage with a substantially stronger tendency toward monogamy; they are far less likely to have been promiscuous before marriage or to engage in extramarital affairs (see chapter 4). In addition, having more traditional views that clearly define sex roles probably reduces the conflict and tension in a marriage. Moreover, being active in a church or synagogue surrounds couples with other couples who also are far less likely to get divorced, which sets an example. Finally, many congregations provide free marriage counseling.

CHILD REARING

Religious differences in child rearing begin at birth. Religious women—Protestants, Catholics, and Jews—are more likely than irreligious mothers to nurse their infants.[14] Subsequently, religious couples do a superior job of raising their children, as is demonstrated by warmer parent-child relationships, closer supervision and more responsible discipline, far lower delinquency rates of their children, and their much greater concern with their children's schooling.

Parent-Child Relationships

Over the years, a number of studies have reported that the more religious college students feel closer to their parents.[15] Then came an unusually definitive study of mother-child relationships based on reports of the degree of closeness as rated by both mother and child, over a period of twenty-four years.[16] Lisa Pearce of Pennsylvania State University and William Axinn of the University of Michigan used data from a random sample of 867 white families in the Detroit metropolitan area who had a child born in 1961. Mothers were interviewed in 1961, 1963, 1966, 1977, 1980, and 1985. Sons and daughters were interviewed in 1980 and again in 1985. The major findings were as follows:

► The more frequent the mother's church attendance, the closer the mother-child relationship, as reported from both sides.

► The greater the importance that mothers place on religion has an even stronger positive effect on mother-child relations than does church attendance.

- The higher the church attendance rates of *both* mothers and children has an even greater positive effect on mother-child relations than does the mother's attendance alone.
- The greater the importance placed on religion by *both* mothers and children has an even greater positive effect on mother-child relations than does the importance placed on religion by mothers alone.
- If children seldom or never attend church, the mother-child relationship is weaker regardless of the frequency of mother's attendance.
- When children place little importance on religion, the mother-child relationship is weaker regardless of the frequency of mother's attendance.

One reason for these religious effects is that the more frequently parents attend church, the warmer and more expressive is their style of parenting.[17] Fathers who attend church more frequently are more likely to praise and hug their children.[18] An extensive study has revealed that religion strongly influences fathers' involvement in youth-related activities, such as coaching sports teams or leading Scout troops.[19]

Perhaps the most elaborate study of the effects of religion on father-child relations was conducted by Valarie King of Pennsylvania State University. Based on a national sample, she identified nearly seven hundred men in their first marriage who had at least one child. King developed five measures of the quality of father-child relationships. Her finding: "Religious fathers are more involved fathers."[20]

Analysis based on another national survey, this one involving a sample of adolescents, by Mark Regnerus of the University of Texas measured their satisfaction with their family on the basis of three factors: how well they felt their family understood them, how much fun they had with their family, and how much they felt that their family paid attention to them.[21] The results:

- The more often their parents attended church, the more satisfied teenagers were with their family.

▸ The greater the importance their parents placed on religion, the more satisfied teenagers were with their family.

▸ If their parents were conservative Protestants, teenagers were more satisfied with their family.

▸ The more often teenagers attended church, the more satisfied they were with their family.

▸ The greater the importance teenagers placed on religion, the more satisfied they were with their family.

▸ These relationships held equally strongly for both male and female teenagers.

Supervision

Notice that in the study by Mark Regnerus reported just above, none of the three measures of teenagers' satisfaction with their families involved freedom from parental supervision. However, the teenagers also were asked whether their parents did or did not let them make their own decisions about the time when they "must be home on weekend nights, the people you hang around with, what you wear, what you eat, how much television you watch, which television programs you watch, and when you go to bed on week nights." It may surprise many that the *less* that they were allowed to make their own decisions on these matters, the more satisfied teenagers were with their family life—probably not because they wanted less supervision, but because they perceived supervision as but another aspect of their parents' involvement and affection. In any event, parental religiousness was strongly related to supervision in this study. Another study conducted by Christian Smith, then at the University of North Carolina, found similar results. As he explained, religious parents "manifest . . . greater amounts of supervision of their children's lives than parents who are less religiously involved."[22]

Discipline

It is depressing to read the "research" showing that children who were spanked experience all sorts of psychological ills and pathological behavior in later life.[23] And it is offensive to read how spanking is a form of child abuse, mainly administered by ignorant parents who are misguided by their religious beliefs.[24] Much of the so-called research involves nonsamples of people with problems, who, when asked, recall having been spanked in childhood and then are guided into blaming that for their current situation. There are no comparisons with well-adjusted people. Other studies lump spanking with severe beatings and even threats or assaults with guns or knives and then "discover" negative effects.[25] As for offensive, consider only the title of Donald Capps's presidential address to the Society for the Scientific Study of Religion: "Religion and Child Abuse: Perfect Together."[26]

Well-done research on religion and discipline reveals the following:[27]

- ► More frequent church attenders are more willing to approve of spanking children.
- ► Active members of conservative Protestant denominations are more approving of child spanking.
- ► More frequent church attenders are more likely than the less religious to spank their children.
- ► Active members of conservative Protestant denominations are more likely than members of other denominations to spank their children.
- ► There is nothing to suggest that these spankings are severe or abusive.
- ► Active members of conservative Protestant denominations are less likely to yell and shout at their children.[28]

Keep in mind that despite being more likely to spank, conservative Protestant parents enjoy closer relationships with their children.

Delinquency

Chapter 2 gave extensive attention to the effects of adolescent religiousness on delinquency. Recently, it became possible to include the effects of parental religiousness and child-rearing practices on their children's delinquency. This is the same study by Mark Regnerus noted above, based on a national sample of adolescents who were interviewed and reinterviewed over several years and whose parents also were interviewed twice. The results showed that parental church attendance and parents belonging to a conservative Protestant denomination both reduced the delinquency of their children, but being a conservative Protestant had the greater effect. In part, the effect of the parents' religiousness was due to their higher level of supervision. But a robust religion effect remained quite independent of supervision, suggesting that religion instills and sustains moral standards that have direct consequences for behavior.

Education

Angry atheists frequently claim that religious folks tend to be uneducated and are inclined to stay that way—putting little value on book learnin'. This fantasy is probably the most outrageous of all regarding people of faith. Americans who never attend church are significantly less likely to have finished high school than are those who attend weekly. Moreover, overwhelming evidence exists that not only do religious people care more than the less religious about their children's education, but they see to it that the children learn more.

Too often, education is equated with school attendance; the more years spent in an educational institution, so the wisdom goes, the greater one's education. That measure is convenient, but very lacking in precision. There are documented cases of college graduates who are unable to read; education is far more accurately measured by tests of what one knows.

As reported in detail in chapter 7, the more religious the student, the better his or her school performance and the higher their achievement scores. This is especially true for African American and Hispanic students. Chapter 7 also assesses the superior performance of students who attend religious schools. Here, too, while all students benefit substantially as compared with their peers at public schools, African American and Hispanic students benefit most.

To conclude this chapter, the focus is on the 1.5 million American students who are being homeschooled—about 3 percent of all American students.

Homeschooling was a minor factor in American education until the 1970s, when several best-selling books advocated abandoning the public schools in favor of teaching children at home. Given widespread dissatisfaction with the results achieved by the public schools (and the great expense of good private schools), growing numbers of American parents began to keep their children home. They did so at some sacrifice, since homeschooling required that one of the couple not be employed outside them home (or at most, employed only part-time).

At first, parents who chose to homeschool their children faced serious opposition from local school authorities, government officials, and the teachers' union; the latter continues to exert intense pressure to force homeschooled children back into the public schools. Various local school boards have been induced to bring legal action against homeschooling parents on grounds that they are violating statutes requiring universal school attendance. Laws against homeschooling were introduced in many state legislatures—without passing. In 1991 the United Nations adopted a Convention on the Rights of the Child which proposes that both spanking and homeschooling be outlawed, and the National Council of Churches immediately began to urge that the United States ratify this convention. (As of 2011 all UN member nations, except the United States and Somalia, have ratified the Convention.) A three-judge panel of the California Court of Appeals ruled as recently as 2008 that homeschooling was illegal unless a parent had a valid teaching credential, which can only be gained by completing the full teacher training course at an accredited college or university. Fortunately for homeschoolers in California, this decision was vacated later in the year.

Meanwhile, a proliferation of educational materials and advice for homeschooling parents began to appear, both in printed form and online. These materials stress the traditional basics of reading, writing, and arithmetic, but also are remarkable for their excellent coverage of history, science, art, and literature. Then it was discovered that homeschooled students excelled.

In 1998, 39,607 homeschooled students were given the Iowa Tests of Basic Skills—if they were below ninth grade—and the older students were given the standardized Tests of Achievement and Proficiency. The data were analyzed by a well-known educational expert, whose report was published in a very respectable social science journal.[29] Here are some of his findings:

- ► On every subject, on every test, and at every grade level, homeschooled students substantially outscored their public and *private* school counterparts.

- ► The above was true despite a bias against the homeschooled students: they were compared with students at their current grade level, regardless of age, despite the fact that most homeschooled students were studying well above the grade level normal for their age. That is, a 10-year-old homeschooled student working with fifth-grade materials was compared with other fifth-graders (who were 11), not with other 10-year-olds.

- ► On average, homeschooled children in grades one through four perform one grade above their public and private school counterparts.

- ► Then the gap widens so rapidly that by the eighth grade, the average homeschooled student performs at four grade levels above the national average—that is, eighth-graders perform at the level of high school graduates.

▶ The more years a student is homeschooled, the higher his or her achievement scores.

All of this explains a remarkable shift. Initially, college admissions officials took a dim view of homeschooled applicants—even when they had outstanding SAT scores. No longer. Now admissions officials regard homeschooled applicants as the cream of the crop.

Who homeschools their children? In the above study, a questionnaire was given to each homeschooling parent, with the results revealing the following information:

▶ More than 80 percent have attended college.

▶ Nearly two-thirds (62 percent) have three or more children.

▶ Three-fourths of homeschooling mothers do not work outside the home, and nearly all who do work are employed only part-time.

▶ Homeschoolers greatly limit the amount of time their children watch television—only 1.6 percent of homeschooled fourth-graders watch more than three hours of TV a day, compared with 40 percent of fourth-graders nationwide.

▶ Sixty-five percent of homeschooling parents belong to a conservative Protestant denomination.

Why do they do it? In 2007 the U.S. Department of Education conducted a nationwide survey of homeschooling parents. The three main reasons they gave for homeschooling were as follows:

▶ Eighty-five percent said they were concerned about the school environment—about safety, drugs, and negative peer pressure.

▶ Seventy-two percent desired to provide religious or moral instruction.

▶ Sixty-eight percent cited dissatisfaction with the academic quality of the schools.

The homeschooling movement is based on religious parents who are so deeply concerned about their children that they are willing to devote many hours a week to providing them with an adequate education.

CONCLUSION

What are the contributions of religion to American family life? Happier marriages and less divorce. More children—enough more that our population is not shrinking. In addition, religious parents are better parents, who raise better-behaved and better-educated children.

* 4 *

Sexuality

IT IS WIDELY assumed, even in liberal religious circles, that traditional Christian attitudes toward sex are utterly repressive: "inflicting shame, guilt, repression and punishment on human sexuality—especially on women's sexuality."[1] Consequently, an Episcopalian priest wrote in a Methodist journal that "the Churches are in danger of evolving into havens for the sexually suppressed."[2] His concern was quite in keeping with the example set by Episcopalian bishop Jane Dixon, who, at her church's General Convention, sported a large button reading, "SEXUALITY, NOT SPIRITUALITY."[3]

Such critics often claim that the New Testament only grudgingly accepts even marital sex and claim to prove this by quoting St. Paul (1 Corinthians 7:9) that "it is better to marry than to burn," as the King James Version put it. Many have claimed that Paul was saying here that sex outside of marriage dooms one to burn in hell. Nothing of the sort! As the Revised Standard Version clarifies, "It is better to marry than to be aflame with passion." Worse yet, the critics remain ignorant of, or are at least unwilling to quote, what Paul really thought about marriage and sex: "The husband should give to his wife her conjugal rights, and likewise the wife to the husband. For the wife does not rule over her own body, but the husband does; likewise the husband does not rule over his own body, but the wife does. Do not refuse one another except perhaps by agreement for a season, that you may devote yourselves to prayer; but come together again, lest Satan tempt you through lack of self-control" (1 Corinthians 7:3–5). Admittedly, even this would not pacify those who think there should be few, if any, limits on sex.

SEXY PURITANS

The constant effort to depict Christianity as hostile to sexual passion often draws upon the Puritans as prime examples. Bertrand Russell merely repeated the common wisdom when he noted the Puritan "determination to avoid the pleasures of sex."[4] This is also ignorant nonsense. Puritan pastors and congregations openly supported a wife's right to orgasms! During the seventeenth century, when James Mattock's wife complained first to her pastor and then to the entire congregation that her husband was not sexually responsive to her, the members of the First Church of Boston expelled him for denying conjugal "fellowship unto his wife for a space of two years together."[5] In fact, court records for the years 1639 to 1711 reveal that about one of every six divorce petitions filed by women "involved charges of male sexual incapacity."[6] Nor was the complaint that their husbands' incapacity denied them children, but that they were denied sexual satisfaction. This point is not only obvious in that many of the women plaintiffs were well past childbearing age, but the issue was stated clearly in open court. Thus, Mary Drury complained to the court in 1658 that her husband Hugh was "Under Some inability of Body" and that he was but a "pretended husband."[7] Mary Heard testified that her husband could not produce an erection: "His yard [penis] Is as weake as a pece of flesh without bone or sinnow. . . . I have beine helpful to him as many times as I could and nevere refused but when the Custom of a woman was upon mee."[8]

Nor was impotence the only grounds the courts recognized for female dissatisfaction. John Williams's wife was granted a divorce on her complaint of his "refuysing to perform marriage duty unto her."[9] Indeed, it was widely agreed that husbands who failed to sexually gratify their wives bore primary responsibility for the wife's extramarital affairs. Elizabeth Jerrad was granted a divorce and exonerated of adultery because of her husband's inattention, the court ruling to "release her from her matrimoniall tye to sayd Robert Jarrad that so she may allso be freed from such temptation as hath occasioned her gross & scandolouse fall into the sinn of uncleaness."[10] New England courts consistently "upheld the view that women had a right to expect 'content and satisfaction' in bed."[11]

Such views involving dissatisfied women are fully supported by the remarkably frank admissions made by satisfied Puritan women, who frequently wrote of "voluptuous swoonings and sweet and subtle pains."[12] Thus, Margaret Durkham, wife of a celebrated clergymen, wrote in a preface to her husband's posthumously published work on the Song of Solomon of her "love-faintings . . . high delights . . . [and] love-languishings" as well as of her delight in "those bashful, but beautiful blushings [and] humble hidings . . . on the Bride's part."[13]

Also contrary to the conventional wisdom, sex manuals were popular among the Puritans. These publications were quite frank and all agreed that husbands owed their wives good sex, being fully aware of female orgasms. Indeed, in this era it was believed that conception was far less likely to occur if the woman did not have an orgasm.[14] Even medical texts as well as sex manuals taught that both men and women produce seed that had to mix in order for conception to occur. That could not happen without female orgasm, which required that the woman be sexually aroused. As one manual put it, the womb, 'skipping as it were for joy,' produced seed 'in that pang of pleassure.'"[15] Thus, in his widely read Domesticall Duties (1622), William Gouge recommended "mutual dalliances for pleasure's sake . . . that husband and wife mutually delight each in the other."[16]

No wonder that informed recent historians, especially those who focus on the family and gender roles, now regard the Puritans as admirable for the stress they placed on romantic sentiments between husbands and wives.[17] This conclusion is fully supported not only by all the facts about marital sex revealed above, but by the abundance of expressions of marital love that fill the surviving sermons, diaries, and letters from that era. Even that pillar of Puritan rectitude, Cotton Mather, wrote this about his wife: "a most lovely creature and such a gift of Heaven to me . . . that the sense thereof dissolves me into tears of joy."[18]

There was nothing heretical about the positive views of marital love and sex that typified the Puritans; they were quite in keeping with St. Paul's advice to couples. Hence, to say that contemporary Christian attitudes about sex are like those of the Puritans is to assert that Christians have very positive attitudes toward sex. And they do, as is reflected in survey studies of members as well as by the abundant Christian marriage manuals.

Of course, Christianity doesn't embrace all manifestations of sexuality. There is serious disapproval of promiscuity, adultery, and to a lesser degree, premarital sex. But does it really matter these days what the churches teach about sex?

PREMARITAL SEX

Promiscuity is rising among younger, unmarried Americans. A very trustworthy national study recently found that 46 percent of unmarried males ages 18–23 reported having had four or more sex partners, as did 45 percent of the unmarried females. Fifteen percent of the males and 10 percent of the females reported eleven or more partners, while 16 percent of both sexes claimed to be virgins.[19] Before birth control pills became widely available in the 1960s and before abortion became legal shortly thereafter, a primary reason that unmarried Americans abstained from intercourse was fear of pregnancy. In those days, most premarital sex was limited to quite serious relationships—very often subsequent to having become engaged. With the fear of pregnancy removed, not only do serious relationships now usually involve sex, but often so do very casual encounters.

"Hooking up" is the widely used term for casual intercourse, and a substantial number of young, single Americans routinely do so. Meanwhile, the dating scene is dying. A national survey of college women conducted in 2001 found that only 55 percent of coeds reported they had been asked out on a date at least six times by the time they were seniors;[20] despite this, dating is far more common among those who attend college. Instead of dating, many young people now hang out in public places and meet at parties. Even so, most young Americans have not hooked up—it being most prevalent at the elite private universities à la Tom Wolfe's thinly concealed account of sexual norms at Duke University in *I Am Charlotte Simmons* (2004).

While there has been a substantial increase in premarital promiscuity, there have been even greater increases in the incidence of oral and anal sexual practices. Among never-married 18- to 23-year-olds, 78 percent of the men and 79 percent of the women report they have engaged in oral sex. The prevalent view is that this is somehow less intimate and serious than intercourse. In addition, 24 percent of the men and 25 percent of the women reported having had anal sex.[21]

Church attendance has a huge impact on engaging in either of these sex practices. For girls ages 15–17, among those who attend weekly, only 13 percent have given oral sex compared with 47 percent of girls who never attend. The same comparison among boys is 13 percent and 43 percent. As for anal sex, 1.5 percent of girls who attend weekly (and 1.2 percent of boys) have had anal sex, while 15 percent of girls (and 17 percent of boys) who never attend have had it.[22]

By far the strongest factors influencing not engaging in

premarital sex at all are church attendance and the importance
one places in religion.[23]

Chastity Pledging

These patterns are, of course, precisely what most church leaders would hope to achieve. In recent years there has been an
increasing emphasis, especially in the more conservative Christian denominations, on chastity. In 1993 a chastity-pledge
movement, True Love Waits, was initiated by the Southern Baptists. By now, millions of American adolescents have pledged as
follows:

> Believing that true love waits, I make a commitment
> to God, myself, my family, my friends, my future
> mate, and my future children to a lifetime of purity
> including sexual abstinence from this day until they
> day I enter a Biblical marriage relationship.

In 1995 Denny Pattyn, an evangelical youth minister in Yuma,
Arizona, developed an elaborate setting for chastity pledges,
now known as the Silver Ring Thing. Pattyn's ceremony most
closely resembles a rock concert: blaring music, intense lighting
effects, videos, and a heavy-duty faith-based message of abstinence. Before the event begins, attendees purchase simple silver
rings to be worn on the ring finger of the left hand until replaced
by a wedding band. Toward the end of the celebration, participants repeat a vow of chastity and slip on their rings. By now,
hundreds of thousands of teenagers have taken part, including
some celebrities.

From the beginning, abstinence pledging has come under
vicious attacks from the usual suspects (ranging from professional sexologists to 'comedian' Bill Maher), and these critics
have dominated the media. Abstinence programs are widely
claimed to be not merely ineffective but harmful. Many sexolo-

gists charge that chastity is unhealthy, causing sexual repression and guilt. Worse yet, a widely cited study claims to show that abstinence is a direct cause of violent behavior, including war. Remarkably, this study was published in the *Bulletin of the Atomic Scientists*, a journal well-known for its hysterical predictions of a coming nuclear holocaust, but having no editors qualified in social science research. Hence, James W. Prescott's paper "Body Pleasure and the Origins of Violence" was given eleven pages to propose that sexual pleasure inhibits violence— "How many of us feel like assaulting someone after we have just experienced an orgasm?"[24] Much of the paper was devoted to data based on a questionnaire given to ninety-six college students and to correlations between items claiming to measure violence, such as support for capital punishment, and other items claiming to measure unhealthy attitudes toward sex, such as disapproving of nudity within the family. These findings have received a great deal of publicity and little or no criticism. However, the primary charge leveled against abstinence pledges was that they didn't work.

Then, in 2001, came a major study of the effectiveness of abstinence pledges, conducted by Peter S. Bearman, a distinguished Columbia University sociologist, and Hannah Brückner, his Yale University colleague. A huge national sample of more than 15,000 students were interviewed three times, twice while they were in high school and a third time after they were young adults. During the first interview they were asked if they had ever pledged to remain chaste until marriage, and 289 reported that they had. After a careful statistical analysis to rule out possible confounding factors, the authors reported that the pledgers subsequently were "much less likely" to have begun having sexual intercourse.[25]

The results were published in the *American Journal of Sociology*, one of the most prestigious social science journals. But these findings received almost no media coverage. Worse yet, when an early draft of this study was presented at a Planned Parenthood workshop in New York City, the president of the Sexuality Information and Education Council of the United States rose and led the crowd in taunting the authors by chanting, "Abstinence programs do not work!"[26]

Ten years later came the findings these critics had been longing for, from a study conducted by Janet Elise Rosenbaum, a new PhD serving as a postdoctoral fellow at Johns Hopkins University. Amazingly, this study was based on the very same national three-wave survey as the one above, but instead of using standard statistical techniques to eliminate the effects of other factors that influence sexual behavior, Rosenbaum used a matching technique.[27] Thus, the 289 pledgers were closely matched on social characteristics such as sex, race, family background, religious participation, and conservative values, with 645 other students from the survey who said they had not taken an abstinence pledge (why the two sets did not include equal numbers, the matching having been done one-to-one, was not explained). The purpose of the matching was to isolate the effects of abstinence pledges from other factors—a substitute for using the standard statistical regression techniques as the previous researchers had done. Perhaps for this reason, the report of her findings was not published in a social science journal. Instead, her paper appeared in a medical journal whose reviewers probably were rather less sophisticated about the analysis of nonexperimental data. In any event, when this researcher compared the pledgers with their "matches," she found that both groups were equally likely to report having engaged in premarital sexual intercourse.

In contrast to the initial study reporting positive effects, these negative findings were widely reported, not only in the mainstream media but even in publications such as *Christianity Today*. In fact, if one checks out "abstinence pledges" online, scores of references to this negative study turn up, and none to the study finding positive effects.

Many social scientists, myself included, would place far greater confidence in the positive findings on grounds of much better analysis. But whatever the truth about the effectiveness of abstinence pledging, no reputable study has ever questioned that religiousness has a substantial influence on premarital sexual behavior. A very creative recent study has revealed some interesting things about how this religiousness effect is magnified or minimized.

Peer Influences

In a sense, survey studies artificially treat respondents as isolated individuals. For example, having selected a national sample of girls ages 15–17, each respondent is sorted out as to her frequency of church attendance. Then the sexual activity of each is examined, and the finding is reported that a girl who attends church weekly is more likely than a nonattender to be a virgin on her wedding day. In reality, of course, every girl in the sample lives in a social world and is influenced not only by her own religious participation but by the religious and sexual lives of her friends. She also influences her friends; in fact she even may shift her friendships to bring them into line with her own attitudes and behavior.

To explore the interaction between individuals and their friends as to when to begin engaging in sexual intercourse, Amy Adamczyk, a young sociology professor at the City University of New York, drew upon the remarkable three-wave national sample of youth used in the two studies of chastity-pledging discussed above. (It is customary in social science for many different studies to be based on a single large survey, and dozens of studies are based on this one, partly because such surveys are extremely expensive and partly because they include so much data that exhausting their research potential is difficult. In this instance, Adamczyk's purposes were served by the fact that the sample had been selected using a cluster technique in which high schools were randomly selected, and then all students in each of the sampled schools were interviewed.) In the first wave of interviews, each student was asked to name up to five best friends. Since most of those named attended the same school as the respondent, Adamczyk could link nearly all students to his or her best friends and summarize the characteristics of these friends as to religiousness, sexual activity, and the like. The question about best friends was reasked in the second wave so that it was possible to identify changes in a respondent's friendship network.

Adamczyk's findings were as follows:

- ► The more religious the teenager, the later he or she began to engage in sexual intercourse. Many still had not yet done so by the end of the third wave of interviews.
- ► The more religious the teenager, the longer the delay between first and second intercourse.
- ► The more religious a teenager's friends, the stronger the delaying effect of his or her own religiousness on their sexual activity. Conversely, having less religious friends reduces the effect of the individual's religiousness.
- ► Religious teenagers who refrain from sex tend to shift their friendships to others who also are religious and chaste. Conversely, when religious teenagers begin having sex they tend to shift to less religious friends.

It follows that church programs that influence the formation of religious friendship networks are more effective in limiting premarital sex than programs that limit their attention to individuals.

MARITAL SEX

Most sexual activity in America takes place in the bedrooms of married couples. This is not merely because most adults are married, but because married couples have sex far more often than do the unmarried. A large national survey found that a third of single women and 23 percent of single men had not had sex in the past year, compared with 1 percent of married men and 3 percent of married women. In contrast, 43 percent of married men reported having sex at least three or four times a week, compared with 26 percent of unmarried men; the same comparison among women was 40 percent versus 20 percent.[28]

Keep these facts in mind, because the major source of data on sex in America seldom distinguishes between the married and unmarried. The National Health and Social Life Survey was conducted in 1992 and involved personal interviews with a national sample of 3,432 Americans 18 years of age and older.[29] The survey is remarkable for the care that went into its execution, and the results are probably very accurate. Unfortunately, although respondents were asked how often they attended religious services, this measure of religiousness was only used in relation to having same-sex partners. In all other applications, religious effects were limited to differences among: Type I Protestants (belonging to a "liberal" denomination), Type II Protestants (belonging to a "conservative" denomination), Catholics, Other, and None; there were too few Jews among the respondents to provide a stable basis for percentaging. In addition, there was little analysis of the data. Nevertheless, the findings are quite informative.

Frequency and Satisfaction

Since Protestants who identify themselves with a conservative denomination are more frequent church attenders than those who identify with a liberal body, and those who give their religious preference as "none" are undoubtedly not very religious, these nominal categories can be used as a crude measure of religiousness. The findings were as follows:

- ► Conservative Protestants (men and women) reported having sex more often than any other group, while liberal Protestants had sex least often. Those without religion were next to lowest in their frequency of sex.
- ► Conservative Protestant women were far more likely than

others to "always" have an orgasm during sex with their husbands (or live-in partner), while those without a religious affiliation were by far the least likely to do so.

▶ Another study based on married, observant, American Orthodox Jewish women found that they had intercourse more frequently than did the average married American woman (as reported in the survey above) and about as frequently as conservative Protestant wives.[30]

▶ Given the above, it is not surprising that conservative Protestant women were far more likely than others to report that they were "extremely" physically satisfied with their sex lives; the irreligious were least likely to give that response.

▶ Conservative Protestant women also were the group most likely to say they were "extremely" emotionally satisfied with their sex lives, and here, too, the irreligious were the least likely to give that answer.

Subsequent to the publication of these findings, two other researchers obtained access to the data and produced an extensive analysis of the basis for emotional and physical satisfaction within sexual unions. Using attendance at worship services rather than denomination as their measure, they found that religiousness had a strong, positive effect.[31] This confirmed an earlier finding based on women who responded to a mail survey conducted by *Redbook* magazine.[32]

Sexual Practices

Although religious American couples have sex more often, achieve greater satisfaction, and are just as likely as the less religious to engage in conventional foreplay such as stimulating the woman's breasts or one another's sexual organs,[33] religious couples are much less apt to engage in sexual practices other than vaginal intercourse. The authoritative National Health and Social Life Survey cited above found as follows:

- ► Conservative Protestants were far less likely to have masturbated in the past year, while the irreligious were those most likely to have done so.
- ► Conservative Protestants were far less likely to have ever given their partners oral sex. The irreligious were the most likely to have done so.
- ► Conservative Protestants were far less likely to have ever received oral sex from their partners. The irreligious were the most likely to have done so.
- ► Conservative Protestants were the least likely to ever have engaged in anal sex. The irreligious were by far the most likely to have done so.

Extramarital Sex

A search of the literature on extramarital sex reveals a surprise: recent studies ignore religiousness altogether. Thus, a lengthy review of the research literature did not even mention religion, although it considered the influence of conservative politics.[34] Given the tone of the articles, I surmise that the neglect of religion is because the researchers disapprove of moral objections to infidelity, being concerned mainly with its consequences for divorce, marital discord, and feelings of guilt. It surely is no surprise that the most powerful predictor of engaging in extramarital sex is premarital promiscuity. Given that religion has been so ignored, it seems surprising that one of the only studies to include religion, and based on a reliable national sample, found that the religious effect on extramarital sex was only slightly weaker than that of premarital promiscuity.[35]

Throughout the 1990s the General Social Surveys asked married people a question about having engaged in extramarital sex. Just as the question about having been picked up by the police was ignored by criminologists (chapter 2), these valuable data seem to have been ignored by social scientists who study sexual behavior.

Table 4.1 is based on a combination of seven GSS surveys. It clearly demonstrates that religiousness has a very strong impact on extramarital sex. People who never attend church are twice as likely to have had extramarital sex than people who attend church weekly. Among women, 7 percent of weekly attenders and 14 percent of never attenders have strayed. Among males the comparison is 14 percent versus 23 percent.

TABLE 4.1. PERCENTAGE OF MARRIED AMERICAN ADULTS WHO HAVE HAD EXTRAMARITAL SEX

Church Attendance	All	Women	Men
Weekly	9%	7%	14%
Sometimes	14%	11%	18%
Never	19%	14%	23%

Source: Calculated by the author from the General Social Surveys 1991; 1993; 1994; 1996; 1998; 2000; 2002.

MORAL COMMUNITY EFFECTS

Church membership rates influence the prevalence of sexually related phenomena in American cities.[36]

- ▸ The higher a city's church membership rate, the lower its rape rate.
- ▸ The higher a city's church membership rate, the lower its rate of sexually transmitted diseases, which, of course, is an indirect measure of the prevalence of promiscuity.

CONCLUSION

Obviously many stereotypes about the sex lives of religious Americans are ill-founded. Religiousness does delay premarital sex, but without any of the lasting repressive effects proclaimed by so many sexperts. That point seems clear in that, once they have married, religious Americans, and especially women, have superior sex lives; they have sex more often, more reliably achieve orgasms, and express greater emotional and physical satisfaction with sex. That they are substantially less apt to masturbate, to have anal and oral sex, or to engage in extramarital affairs would not seem to be discreditable.

* 5 *

Mental and Physical Health

FOR MOST of the twentieth century, anyone who proposed positive religious effects on mental and physical health was dismissed as a religious fanatic or a quack. The famous experts in mental health, including pioneers such as Sigmund Freud and Albert Ellis, denounced religion not only as a primary *cause* of mental illness, but as a *form* of mental illness. Freud condemned religion as a "sweet—or bittersweet—poison," a "neurosis," an "intoxicant," and "childishness to be overcome" all on one page of his famous *Future of an Illusion* (1927)—the "illusion" in his title referred to religion, of course.[1] Ellis published a list of eleven psychological "pathologies" resulting from religion[2] and claimed that the effective "therapeutic solution to [these] emotional problems is to be quite unreligious."[3]

In the 1960s everyone's favorite psychologist of religion was Harvard's Gordon W. Allport.[4] He redefined the field by identifying two kinds of religiousness: intrinsic and extrinsic. *Intrinsic* religiousness is very mild in terms of intensity, very vague as to its beliefs, and subject to continuing and constructive doubts—a form of religion, according to Allport, that is suitable for mature, intelligent adults. *Extrinsic* religion involves firm belief and is, therefore, a form of "primitive credulity"; he also described extrinsic religion as "childish, authoritarian, and irrational."[5] Allport believed it possible for intrinsic religion to be compatible with good mental health, but held that extrinsic religion was essentially a form of mental illness and was associated with many other forms of mental aberration as well.

Freud, Ellis, and Allport were not lonely voices. Theirs were the accepted views throughout the psychological trades. Hence, no one turned a hair when Mortimer Ostow solemnly testified that Evangelical Protestantism is merely regression "to the state of mind of the child who resists differentiation from its mother."[6] Michael P. Carroll's claim that praying the rosary is "disguised gratification of repressed anal erotic desires"—a substitute for playing "with one's feces"— was published in a leading journal.[7] Indeed, anyone who suggested there might be positive religious effects on mental or physical health risked being identified as a witchdoctor or, worse yet, a believer.

Then came a revolution in medical and psychiatric perspectives. It began as a few researchers confronted evidence that was incompatible with the prevailing antireligious certitudes. My colleague Jeff Levin recalls that during the 1980s, "Those of us actively investigating the linkages between religion and health could have fit around a conference table. A very small one."[8] I am delighted to be included as an early player in this revolution because of a paper I published reporting evidence that religiousness was correlated with better mental health.[9] But the truth is that my paper was a onetime effort, and this enormous new scientific literature was built without my help. A summary volume of new research findings, published in 2001, required 712 pages.[10] Since then the body of research on religion and health has grown so rapidly that the second edition, published in 2012, ran to 1,192 pages.

MENTAL HEALTH

Given the certainty expressed by so many psychologists and psychiatrists that authentic religiousness either is mental illness per se, or that it makes people highly vulnerable to personality problems, one might suppose that there was a substantial body of research pointing in this direction. The truth is that these "experts" usually testified with no research evidence at all, and relied entirely on their clinical insights and personal convictions. As it turns out, they not only were wrong to blame mental illness on religion but were doubly wrong for failing to realize that religiousness provides substantial protection against mental illness. It even can make people happier.

Happiness

Philosophers have long wrestled with the notion of happiness. Aristotle proposed that "happiness is the meaning and the purpose of life, the whole aim and end of human existence."[11] Serious and sustained research on the social correlates of happiness began at the National Opinion Research Center (NORC) at the University of Chicago in 1960 under the direction of Norman Bradburn. After a series of studies, Bradburn and his colleagues decided that a single question was a sufficient and valid measure of happiness: "Taken all together, how would you say things are these days—would you say that you are very happy, pretty happy, or not too happy?" This item was subsequently included in the first General Social Survey (GSS) when it was conducted by NORC in 1972 and has appeared in twenty-three GSS studies since then (the last time in 2002). Each GSS is based on personal interviews of a random sample of the adult American population, conducted by NORC.

Indicative that the item taps a basic sentiment and that it does not reflect momentary matters is the fact that only once between 1972 and 2002 did the percentage of "very happy" respondents dip below 30 percent (29 percent in 1994) and only once did it exceed 35 percent (38 percent in 1974). Such small variations are entirely within the confidence limits of the samples and must be dismissed as meaningless, random fluctuations. That means, of course, that wars, recessions, Watergate, the attacks of

September 11, 2001, and other such wrenching public events had no impact on personal happiness, suggesting that people define it as an entirely private affair.

Unfortunately, no one bothered to examine the link between religiousness and happiness based on these fine data, until a graduate student and I did so in 2008—thirty-six years after the first national data were collected.[12] What makes this even odder is that, although these data were available to anyone without cost, during these same years a number of studies of religion and happiness were published, but all were based on nonsamples such as "some adult students of education," or residents of "northern Wisconsin." In fact, most of these studies were based on groups of elderly respondents. Even so, all of them found a positive religious effect on happiness.[13]

When Jared Maier and I pooled all twenty-four GSS surveys that included the happiness item, the results were as shown in Table 5.1. The more often that Americans attend church, the more likely they are to be happy. Reading across the table we see that 40 percent of the weekly attenders say they are very happy compared with 25 percent of those who never attend. Conversely, those who never attend (18 percent) are twice as likely to say they are not too happy as are those who attend weekly (9 percent). Religion matters. Extensive analyses of these same data revealed that the church attendance effect remained strong within categories of race, sex, income, and education.

Authoritarianism

The publication of *The Authoritarian Personality* in 1950 by a group of scholars at the University of California, Berkeley, was greeted with extraordinary enthusiasm by social scientists. Several of the authors were radical Marxists who had been members of the Frankfurt School, and who had fled from Germany to the United States following Hitler's seizure of power. The project began as an attempt to understand the Nazi mind,

TABLE 5.1. CHURCH ATTENDANCE AND HAPPINESS

	Church Attendance		
	Weekly	Sometimes	Never
Very happy	40%	28%	25%
Pretty happy	51%	59%	57%
Not too happy	9%	13%	18%
Total	100%	100%	100%

Source: General Social Surveys, combined years.

hence the authors originally had planned to title their book *The Fascist Character and the Measurement of Fascist Trends.* Upon the advice of their publisher they switched to the less obviously political term, "authoritarianism." However, they continued to identify the scale they constructed to measure their central concept as the F-scale, short for Fascism scale.

As developed by the authors, authoritarianism refers to rigidities in the personality structure of individuals: an inability to tolerate ambiguity and ambivalence. These structures are said to be laid down in childhood by particular kinds of training and experience. The dominant line taken by the book was to condemn all forms of conservative (or less than radical) political views, as well as religion, as the sources and products of this mental abnormality, while praising all forms of leftism as liberating and rational. Even back then, this struck a most responsive chord in academia, and revelations that authoritarianism lurked behind most conventional beliefs became de rigueur. By now, literally thousands of articles on authoritarianism have been published in social science journals, nearly all of them remarkably trivial—from reactions to the Bill Clinton–Monica Lewinsky affair to styles of family budget planning—and nearly always based on nonsamples of college students. But the most remarkable thing of all is that one of the most central and oft-repeated claims concerning authoritarianism was initially made without any evidence and has lived on despite negative findings.

Among social scientists, "everyone" knows that the authors of *The Authoritarian Personality* presented statistical evidence of a positive correlation between the F-scale and religiousness. Some years ago I asked a dozen prominent social scientists, including one of the book's authors, whether such data had been presented, and all replied that it had. That response shows the power of bias and repetition, since no such evidence appears in the book. All discussions of religion and authoritarianism are in sections of the book based on individual clinical case studies. When I then searched the published research literature on the matter I found a handful of studies, all of them of poor quality, yet all of them reporting that there is *no* relationship between religiousness and the F-scale. I then published an analysis based on a national sample of the adult American population which showed that neither religious beliefs nor church attendance are correlated with the F-scale.[14] I thought that would settle the matter, but I was wrong. As a typical example, the first sentence of an article in a leading journal, published some years after my research appeared, innocently stated, "Previous research has consistently found that religious individuals tend to be authoritarians and authoritarians tend to be religious."[15] Attempting to understand how such claims could continue, I discovered that because so many psychologists are convinced that religion *must* breed authoritarianism, they have changed the measurement of authoritarianism in ways that make such relationship a tautological certainty.[16]

In place of the old notions about authoritarianism and the F-scale came a new concept known as "Right-Wing Authoritarianism" and a new scale.[17] To ensure that this version of authoritarianism must be related to religiousness, the scale includes religious items—For example, "People should pay less attention to the Bible and other traditional forms of religious guidance, and instead develop their own personal standards of what is moral and immoral." Disagree with that statement and one is scored as a Right-Wing Authoritarian. The same for "Atheists and others who have rebelled against the established religion are no doubt every bit as good and virtuous as those who attend church." Many other items are meant to challenge traditional morality, such as "There is nothing wrong with premarital sexual intercourse" and "There is absolutely nothing wrong with nudist camps." Finally, "Students in high school and university must be encouraged to challenge their parents' ways, confront established authorities, and in general criticize the customs and traditions of our society."[18] How could a scale with such items in it *not* be correlated with measures of religiousness such as church attendance? It is tantamount to discovering that religious people are religious. This is not science—not even social science!

Depression

Various forms of depression make up the most common kind of personality problem. This human affliction varies from enduring periods of gloomy outlook to the intense depression that sometimes results in suicide. The immense worldwide sales of antidepressant medications testify to the prevalence of the problem.

Epidemiologists have developed excellent standardized measures of depression that have been used to study general populations. Other research on depression is based on groups manifesting serious symptoms of the affliction. Research on depression has recently given attention to religion.

Recall that Gordon Allport equated extrinsic religion with mental illness, while giving the vague religiousness he identified as intrinsic a clean bill of health. That perspective has prompted many studies, including some on depression. The results of a dozen such studies are as follows:[19]

- ▶ Contrary to Allport, persons who score high on intrinsic religiousness tend to score high on measures of depression.
- ▶ Perhaps even more embarrassing for Allport's supporters, persons who score high on extrinsic religion tend to score low on measures of depression.
- ▶ Those whose religious orientation is extrinsic are only about half as likely to receive a diagnosis of a major depression as are those whose religious orientation in intrinsic.[20]
- ▶ A study of eighty-seven depressed older adults hospitalized for medical illnesses found that those who scored high on extrinsic religiousness recovered from their depressions 70 percent more rapidly than did those scored high on intrinsic religiousness.[21]

Allport had everything backward! Perhaps only in academic settings such as the Harvard faculty club could a vague, watered-down spirituality be mistaken for the real thing.

Of course, many studies of religion and depression did not bother with Allport's notions, but examined the effects of conventional religious beliefs and participation in religious congregations, finding that both offer very substantial protection against depression.[22]

Neurosis

Neurosis identifies a class of mental difficulties and disorders that does not involve delusions and hallucinations, nor does it involve behavior beyond the boundaries of social acceptability. As this definition makes plain, neurosis is a catch-all category for mental health problems less disabling than those associated with terms such as insanity, madness, or psychosis.

My very early study of religion and neurosis began as an attempt to assess the validity of a then-popular interview schedule meant to assess the mental health of a population. First, one hundred patients were randomly selected from all persons currently receiving outpatient treatment at a northern California mental health clinic. Each was matched with his or her nearest neighbor of the same sex, age, race, marital status, and education. Then all two hundred people were interviewed; the interview schedule was presented as a study of physical health, and the interviewers believed that was the case. To test the validity of the interview for identifying persons with mental health problems, analysis was conducted to see how accurately it distinguished those in treatment from their untreated matches. As it turned out, the interview schedule was sufficiently valid to give a reasonably accurate assessment of the mental health needs of a population, but not sufficiently valid to serve as an individual case finder.[23]

Because several questions about religion were included in the interview schedule, I could compare the religiousness of the treatment group with the matching group. The results were strong and compelling.

- ► Sixteen percent of the treatment group said they had no religion, compared with 3 percent of the matching group.
- ► Sixteen percent of the treatment group said religion was "not important to them at all," compared with 4 percent of the matching group.
- ► Fifty-four percent of the treatment group did not belong to a church congregation, compared with 40 percent of the matching group. They all lived just south of San Francisco in the heart of the unchurched belt (see chapter 2).
- ► Twenty-one percent of the treatment group never attended church, compared with 5 percent of the matching group.

All of these differences were highly statistically significant. Those being treated for mental health problems were less religious than the normal population.

In this early paper I also included data from a survey based on a national sample of the adult population. It included two scales designed to measure mental health problems.[24] The first was meant to measure psychic inadequacy. It included items such as "I worry a lot" and "I tend to go to pieces in a crisis." The second scale was devoted to neurotic distrust. Among its items was, "It is safest to assume that all people have a vicious streak and it will come out when they are given a chance," and "Do you think most people can be trusted?" As shown in Table 5.2, both scales are strongly, negatively related to church attendance. Weekly attenders (11 percent) were less than half as likely to score high on psychic inadequacy as were those who never attended (23 percent). Twenty-two percent of weekly attenders scored high on neurotic distrust, compared with 40 percent of those who never attended.

TABLE 5.2. CHURCH ATTENDANCE AND MENTAL HEALTH

| | Church Attendance | | | |
	Weekly	Sometimes	Never	All
High on psychic inadequacy	11%	14%	23%	13%
High on neurotic distrust	22%	24%	40%	24%

Source: Stark 1971.

In the many years since I published these data, the same results have been found again and again on many different measures of neurosis.[25]

Psychosis

The term "psychosis" is applied to a group of psychological conditions often referred to as mental illness or insanity. Victims have abnormal thought processes, many experience hallucinations (unreal sounds, visions, and sensations) and delusions (incorrect beliefs and perceptions), and they often engage in bizarre behavior.

For centuries, religion was commonly regarded as a cause

of psychosis because the hallucinations and delusions of the afflicted often had religious content. The 1860 Census of the United States included all of the nation's mental hospitals, and for each patient the census taker was supposed to record the cause of his or her insanity (in those days such a diagnosis was included in each patient's records). As it turned out, most census takers failed to fulfill this part of their instructions, and causes of insanity were reported for only seventeen of the forty-two mental hospitals then in operation. Examination of these data revealed that 7 percent of all the male patients and 6 percent of all the females were believed to have been driven insane by "religious excitement"—compared with 18 percent of the males and 2 percent of the females whose insanity stemmed from "masturbation."[26] During that era, several well-known experts on mental illness urged that people with weak nervous systems should avoid religious revivals.[27] Of course, all the experts were concerned about preventing masturbation.

Although the notion that religious excitement could cause psychosis was entirely consistent with the views of Freud, Ellis, Allport, and the rest, recent progress in the diagnosis and treatment of psychosis has made any link to religiousness seem impossible. That is, psychosis is now regarded as primarily having physiological rather than psychological causes.[28] So, too, few any longer believe that masturbation drives you crazy.

SUICIDE AND MORAL COMMUNITIES

At the end of the eighteenth century, several European nations began to collect data on the causes of death. When these mortality statistics were assembled, it became possible for the first time to examine the prevalence of suicide. The data revealed two shocking patterns.[29]

First, the number of people who took their own lives was extremely *stable over time*: year after year, in any particular place, nearly identical numbers of people committed suicide. This was so shocking because it forced recognition that what had heretofore been assumed to be a most individual action, rooted in each person's psychology and circumstances, must be greatly influenced by their social environment. Were suicide an idiosyncratic, individual action, it should occur at a random rate and therefore the number of suicides should vary greatly from one time to another. But that was not the case, which testifies to the profoundly social character of human existence.

The second shocking revelation about suicide was that the *rates varied greatly* from one place to another. The suicide rate for Paris was more than four times higher than the rate for London. The rates varied from a high of 34.7 per 100,000 population per year to a low of 0.8 across the eighty-six departments of France. Why? Here, too, the answer had to be social. Something about life in some places must be more conducive to suicide.

Many leading intellectuals, including the celebrated German philosopher Immanuel Kant, realized that these variations required explanations based on characteristics of communities, not individuals, and thus a new social science was needed. Sociology was born.[30]

As time passed, a third aspect of suicide rates was noticed: they were slowly *rising*. The annual suicide rate for Sweden was 6.8 per 100,000 during the decade 1830–1840, but by 1866–1870 it had risen to 8.5. The rate for Paris rose from 34.7 in 1827–1830 to 42.6 in 1872–1876. What could be causing this? In 1879 Henry Morselli, then the leading expert on suicide, offered an explanation: "the growth of suicide is accounted for by the decrease in religious sentiment."[31] Shortly thereafter, the other leading authority on suicide, Thomas Masaryk, agreed: "the modern tendency to suicide has its true cause in the irreligiosity of our time."[32] (I am ignoring Emile Durkheim's famous study of suicide done at this same time because it now is clear that he falsified some of his results and misconceived others.[33])

In keeping with the analysis proposed by Morselli and Masaryk more than a century ago, today most Western European nations, being less religious than America, have suicide rates far higher than that of the United States. The annual American suicide rate hovers around 11.0 per 100,000, compared with 21.1 in Belgium, 20.0 in Finland, 18.0 in France, and 17.4 in Switzerland (the Russian rate is a shocking 34.3).[34]

Contemporary studies of suicide overwhelmingly focus on explaining variations in the rates of geographic units such as nations, states, provinces, and cities. In part this is because it is very difficult to study suicide at the individual level. Obviously, people who commit suicide can't be interviewed, and trying to reconstruct their biographies after their deaths is very expensive and quite inexact. Surveys are limited to studying attitudes toward suicide, which may have very little connection with acts of suicide. Another reason to focus on geographic units has to do with the initial observations of the steadiness of suicide rates and the very great variation in rates from one place to another.

Many studies[35] have been based on the standard metropolitan statistical areas (SMSAs) of the United States—the major cities and their surrounding suburbs. All of these studies reported powerful religious effects: the higher the church membership rate of an SMSA, the lower its suicide rate. This religious effect remains strong even when other factors such as rapid population turnover are taken into account. Thus we not only once again discover the significance of moral communities; studies of suicide in fact first suggested the idea of moral communities.

The early European suicide researchers all believed that Catholics were substantially less likely than Protestants to commit suicide, given that the Catholic Church imposed such a stigma on suicide; persons who took their own lives were deemed guilty of a mortal sin and were denied church funeral services and burial in Catholic cemeteries. However, recent American studies have found that the proportion of church members who are Roman Catholics has no additional impact on suicide. In America, religiousness in general, not a particular brand of religiousness, seems to matter. It has been suggested that the Catholic Church has greatly relaxed its opposition to suicide; those who commit suicide nowadays are usually assumed to have been of unsound mind at that time and thereby qualify to receive church sacraments and burial in Catholic cemeteries. Perhaps so. But reanalysis of the nineteenth-century European data that were thought to show a Catholic effect reveals that no such effect ever existed.[36] Protestant places did not have higher suicide rates than did Catholic places. However, measures of religiousness, such as church attendance, were strongly, negatively related to suicide in Europe during this era as well.[37]

Why does religiousness produce these psychological benefits? A small part may be a selection effect. At least in the United States, being religious is "normal." But the larger part probably reflects the capacity of religion to offer people hope and purpose, and to comfort them in the face of life's disappointments and tragedies. This capacity is greatly amplified by participation in religious congregations, where one is surrounded by a supportive group.

Physical Health

A study of tombstones in ancient Roman cemeteries revealed that early Christians outlived their pagan neighbors.[38] The reason usually given is that the early Christians took care of the sick and the needy, even to the extent of providing effective nursing services during the great plagues that struck the empire.[39] But that does not explain why many careful studies have all found that modern Americans who attend church weekly greatly outlive those who never attend. The best national study suggests that attenders have an average of 7.6 years of greater life expectancy at age 20 than do nonattenders.[40] Most of this difference in life expectancy remains even after removal of the religion-related effects of "clean living."

Obviously, if religion is associated with increased life expectancy, religion also ought to be associated with reduced risks of various physical ailments. And it is.

- A study based on 10,059 Jewish men in Israel found that the more religious they were, the less likely they were to develop a myocardial infarction within five years of their initial examination.[41]

- A study of 232 older American adults who had coronary artery bypass surgery found that those who attended religious services were less than half as likely to die during the follow-up period as were those who never attended (5 percent versus 12 percent). Of those who defined themselves as deeply religious, none died, compared with 11 percent of the others.[42]

- Many studies, done in many nations, have found a very strong negative relationship between religiousness and high blood pressure (hypertension).[43]

- A large study involving 2,812 persons over 65 found that those who attended church (even if not very often) were significantly less likely to have strokes.[44] A number of other studies have confirmed this effect.[45]

EFFORTS TO EXPLAIN

As noted earlier, the positive effects of religion on mental health are not so difficult to explain. First are the direct effects of religious beliefs that offer hope, meaning, and comfort as well as the capacity to dispel guilt by way of confession and forgiveness. As Jeff Levin and Harold Vanderpool put it, religion can "serve to ease dread and anxiety, reduce personal and group tension and aggressiveness, allay fears, and moderate loneliness, depression, anomie, and/or feelings of entrapment and inferiority."[46] Second is the provision of a socially supportive group that can serve as an effective refuge, even for the sad and lonely. In attempting to explain the positive effects of religiousness on physical health, emphasis is placed on the connection between mental and physical health. For example, it is well established that various psychological problems such as anxiety and depression can elevate blood pressure, which, in turn, may result in strokes and heart disease.

And this is where nearly all discussions of how religiousness influences physical health stop. That is, the explanatory model is that religiousness influences mental health directly, and mental health, in turn, influences physical health. No direct effects of religion on physical health are postulated. Most of the literature is pointedly silent on the subject of healing. This is quite understandable, since to discuss healing is to venture over the line separating science from miracles.

On "Miraculous" Cures

Even to propose that religion has indirect effects on physical health through its psychological benefits arouses considerable antagonism in the usual secular circles. Thus, it is no surprise that to propose that religion has the actual power to heal arouses bitter attacks and ridicule. The professional atheist Richard Dawkins derided experimental efforts to test the effects of prayer on the recovery of seriously ill patients as "amusing, if rather pathetic."[47] Nonetheless, Dawkins was careful to cite only a study that failed to find any such effects, failing even to mention that a number of studies have reported such effects—there also are additional studies that found no prayer effects. What strikes me as truly remarkable is that there have been *any* such studies, regardless of outcome, done by qualified researchers at major medical centers.

The first study was conducted by Randolph Byrd, a physician in the coronary care unit of San Francisco General Hospital. Working with a group of nearly four hundred patients, he randomly assigned half of them to be prayed for by a group of Christian volunteers, while the others served as the control group—a classic experimental design. Subsequent examinations found that patients who had been prayed for exhibited beneficial effects.[48]

Since Byrd published in 1988, a number of additional studies have been conducted on the effects of prayer upon healing. A study of AIDS patients found a positive effect.[49] A study of coronary patients at the Mayo Clinic found no prayer effects.[50] A review of seventeen studies published before 2007 reported a small effect in some.[51] Controversy continues.

Many devout Christians are offended by the fundamental assumption on which these studies are based—that prayers are like magical incantations in that they produce results in a mechanical way, or that God is under some sort of compulsion to grant prayers, the more so the larger the number who are praying. As one theologian put it, "The whole exercise cheapens religion and promotes an infantile theology."[52]

In any event, whatever the results of these studies, not only do most Americans believe in miracles, the Baylor National Religion Survey of 2007 found that 23 percent believed they had "witnessed a miraculous, physical healing," and 16 percent reported, "I received a miraculous, physical healing." Of course, this does not prove that such miracles occur, let alone that they are common, but it does prove that many people are convinced that their recovery was God-given and, as is well known among churchgoers, millions of Americans regularly pray for the health and recovery of others. Based on the Baylor National Religion Survey of 2010, 87 percent of Americans say they have prayed "for another person's healing from an illness or injury," and 79 percent have prayed for their own healing. Indeed, 53 percent have "participated in a prayer group, prayer chain, or prayer circle that prayed for other people's healing from illness or injury." In addition, a recent study found that knowledge that others were praying for them significantly improved the mental health of a sample of elderly people.[53]

Table 5.3 compares denominations as to claims to having been healed. Overall, Protestants (19 percent) are somewhat more likely than Catholics (12 percent) to report miraculous healings. Within Protestantism, Evangelicals (27 percent) are most likely to report having been healed, and members of liberal denominations (11 percent) are least likely. Note that 4 percent of those reporting that they have no religion say they have been healed. That reflects that the majority of Americans who say they have no religion do not mean that they are irreligious, but that they do not belong to a church (see chapter 1).

TABLE 5.3. PERCENTAGE WHO SAY THEY HAVE RECEIVED A "MIRACULOUS PHYSICAL HEALING"

Protestant	19%
Evangelical	27%
Nondenominational	18%
Liberal	11%
Roman Catholic	12%
No Religion	4%
All Americans	16%

Source: Baylor National Religion Survey 2007.

Since one needs to be ill before one can be healed, it is no surprise that the proportion who claim to have been healed rises with age, from 12 percent of those under 30, to 22 percent of those age 70 and older. Women (18 percent) were more likely to report being healed than were men (13 percent). There was a very large race effect: 14 percent of whites compared with 37 percent of African Americans. People with postgraduate degrees were less likely (11 percent) to report being healed than were those who had not gone beyond high school (19 percent). This difference was cut in half when race was controlled.

In any event, faith healing is not something found only among small groups of Pentecostal Protestants, but is widely accepted and experienced in all branches of American Christianity.

Conclusion

We know with certainty that religion has strong, positive effects on mental health. Religious people are far less prone to depression and neurosis. We also know with certainty that religious people are physically healthier than the irreligious, since frequent attenders have an average of 7.6 years of longer life expectancy at age 20. But we do not know whether religiousness has any direct effects on physical health or whether its physical effects are entirely a result of superior mental health. Most Americans believe that prayer produces cures, but there is no firm evidence that it does.

* 6 *

Generous Citizenship

WHEN ASKED TO define a good citizen, President Theodore Roosevelt responded, "The first requisite of a good citizen in this Republic of ours is that he shall be able and willing to pull his weight."[1] Pulling one's weight can mean many things, but it certainly includes being generous with one's money and time and playing an active part in community affairs. Many recent critics of religious Americans, and especially of Evangelicals, claim they are poor citizens in that they limit their generosity to their own kind: "Isn't it misleading to give money to your church and call that 'giving to charity'? . . . People who go to church a lot volunteer a lot—but only for the church. . . . Church participation makes them less generous with their time, not more."[2] Many of these same critics go on to condemn religious citizens for being active in community affairs on the grounds they do so only to impose their narrow morality and promote reactionary political policies. Hence, the prominent Kevin Phillips charged that America is rapidly headed toward "disenlightenment" and soon to be a "theocracy."[3]

Nonsense! Religious Americans excel in their generosity and volunteerism, not only to religious groups and causes, but to purely secular ones as well. And contrary to the plethora of fantasies about Evangelical plots to take over the government, church attenders are no more active in politics than are nonattenders, and the same is true for Evangelicals. Moreover, Evangelicals are little different from other Americans in terms of their political opinions, even on the so-called moral issues.

GENEROSITY

All five of the world's major religions stress the moral significance of generosity. The third of the five pillars of Islam is *zakāt*, or almsgiving, and it is thought that those who do not pay *zakāt* will have their prayers rejected. In Buddhism, charity is the first of the six Paramitas, which are the practices by which one pursues perfection. The Torah admonishes Jews that "there shall be no needy among you" (Deuteronomy 15:4). The *Bhagavad-gita* teaches Hindus that there are three paths to breaking the cycle of reincarnation, and the first of these is karma yoga, which involves religious deeds such as charity. And of course, Christianity teaches that the three virtues are "faith, hope, and charity."

But, does it matter? Within each of these religious traditions, are some more religious, more charitable? Yes. My analysis based on the Gallup World Poll—annual surveys of 162 nations to which I am privileged to have access—reveals that in all parts of the world, and within each of the five major faiths, people who "attended a place of worship or religious service in the past seven days" score higher on a generosity index than do nominal members of their faith who had not attended. The index consists of two items:

Have you done any of the following in the past month?

How about donated money to a charity?

How about helped a stranger or someone you didn't know who needed help?

Just because all five major religions seem to produce generosity in their adherents does not mean that all nations enjoy equal levels of individual generosity, if for no other reason than nations differ greatly in their proportions of religious citizens. As we shall see, religion is the basis for the high levels of charitable giving that characterize Americans.

COMPARATIVE GENEROSITY

For nearly a century American generosity has benefitted millions living abroad. Although few Europeans seem to remember or care, twice during the twentieth century American generosity saved their ancestors from bitter famine and misery in the wake of two devastating wars. Following World War I (1914–1918), the American Relief Organization, directed by future president Herbert Hoover, transported immense amounts of food to Europe and spent large sums on public health measures—much of this money was donated by U.S. citizens, and taxpayers provided the rest. World War II (1939–1945) was far more devastating, and U.S. aid was correspondingly far greater. American generosity, much of it channeled through the Marshall Plan, not only fed Europe, but financed the rebuilding of its smashed cities and underwrote its economic recovery. Ever since, America has shared its wealth with many less-developed nations through extensive foreign aid, running to many billions of dollars a year.

Even presuming that charity begins at home, it appears that the affluent Western Europeans are less generous than are Americans. Table 6.1 is based on data collected by the Gallup World Poll, and the generosity index is the same as the one noted above. Respondents received a point for responding that they had given to a charity and another point for having helped a stranger. Thus, scores on the index range from two to zero. The table reports the percent scoring high (two).

Reading down the column headed by "All" we see that the British are as generous as Americans. In both nations 47 percent scored high. But after that, substantial trans-Atlantic differences appear in the table. Thus, in Sweden only 29 percent scored high; in Spain, 17 percent; and in Greece, only 7 percent.

Now look at the two columns headed "Church Attenders" and "Nonattenders." Reading across, we see that in every one of these nations, people who attended a worship service during the past week were substantially more likely to score high on the generosity index than were the nonattenders. In the United

TABLE 6.1. COMPARATIVE GENEROSITY
(Percentage Scored High on Generosity Index)

	Number of Cases	All	Church Attenders	Non-attenders
United States	5,238	47%	55%	39%
United Kingdom	5,244	47%	58%	44%
Austria	4,005	40%	47%	37%
Netherlands	4,001	38%	43%	36%
Switzerland	2,003	37%	44%	34%
Denmark	5,014	36%	41%	35%
Sweden	5,005	29%	41%	27%
Germany	8,255	28%	37%	25%
Norway	2,001	25%	35%	23%
Italy	5,023	25%	29%	21%
Belgium	4,030	24%	32%	21%
Finland	3,015	22%	35%	19%
Spain	5,018	17%	24%	13%
France	5,232	16%	25%	14%
Portugal	4,011	15%	19%	12%
Greece	4,002	7%	10%	5%

Source: Gallup World Poll, combined samples 2006–2011.

States this comparison is 55 percent versus 39 percent; in Sweden it is 41 percent versus 27 percent. Even in Greece, where few scored high, attenders were twice as likely (10 percent) to score high as were nonattenders (5 percent). As can be seen in the first column at the left, the results for each nation are based on a huge number of cases, and therefore all the differences between attenders and nonattenders are statistically significant at the highest level (beyond .000).

Just as America benefits from having lower crime rates than Western Europe, it also benefits from higher levels of generosity. Clearly, too, this advantage is due in part to America's greater religiousness.

AMERICAN RELIGION AND GENEROSITY

In recent years, the average American household has contributed about 5 percent of its income to charitable causes. About two-thirds of this goes to churches and church-related charities; the other third to secular charities.[4] Analysts often claim that religious people mostly limit their giving to their churches, and that the bulk of the donations for secular charitable groups such as the United Way come from less religious Americans. That may be true for some secular causes with religious implications such as Planned Parenthood, but it's not so generally. Despite the substantial amounts they give to religious causes, the more religious Americans are the major source of funding for the secular charities as well. One recent study found that 51 percent of church attenders had given money to a "nonreligious" charity in the past year, compared with 37 percent of nonattenders.[5]

Table 6.2 is based on the General Social Survey of 2002. All respondents were asked whether they had given money to a charity in the past year. Seventy-eight percent of Americans said, "Yes." Eighty percent of Protestants and Catholics said they had done so, as did 96 percent of the Jews (although the small

TABLE 6.2. PERCENTAGE WHO HAVE GIVEN MONEY TO A CHARITY IN THE PAST YEAR

Denomination	
Protestant	80%
Catholic	80%
Jewish	96% (only 24 cases)
None	66%
All	78%

Church Attendance	All	Women	Men	White	African American
Weekly	87%	87%	86%	91%	80%
Sometimes	80%	81%	79%	82%	69%
Never	60%	64%	56%	62%	30%

Source: Computed by the author from the General Social Survey 2002.

number of Jews makes this figure unreliable), but only 66 percent of those saying they had no religion gave money to a charity in the past year. As for the effect of church attendance, 87 percent of the weekly attenders, 80 percent of those who attend less often, and only 60 percent of the nonattenders said they had donated. The effects of church attendance hold up among both men and women, whites and African Americans.

These findings are consistent with a substantial research literature on charitable donations.[6]

VOLUNTEERISM

Americans are also generous with their time and energy. Table 6.3 show the percentages in each nation who answered, "Yes," when asked by Gallup interviewers, "Have you volunteered your time to an organization in the past month?" Forty-three percent of Americans said they had volunteered. Next highest were the Dutch and the Norwegians at 39 percent, and the percentages decline until reaching 6 percent among the Greeks. Reading across, the table also shows that in every nation, church attenders are substantially more likely to volunteer. The number of cases is the same in this table as in Table 6.1; here, too, all of

TABLE 6.3. PERCENTAGE THAT HAVE VOLUNTEERED
THEIR TIME IN THE PAST MONTH

	All	Church Attenders	Nonattenders
United States	43%	57%	31%
Netherlands	39%	55%	34%
Norway	39%	60%	35%
Switzerland	30%	40%	27%
Finland	30%	49%	27%
United Kingdom	29%	46%	24%
Austria	28%	40%	21%
Belgium	27%	39%	23%
France	26%	36%	24%
Germany	25%	38%	19%
Denmark	24%	37%	21%
Italy	19%	24%	14%
Spain	16%	20%	13%
Sweden	14%	25%	12%
Portugal	12%	16%	9%
Greece	6%	8%	4%

Source: Gallup World Poll, combined samples, 2006–2011.

the church attendance comparisons are highly statistically significant. The American results are almost identical with those I found in the 2002 National Election Survey conducted by the University of Michigan: 62 percent of weekly attenders said they had done volunteer work in the past year, compared with 35 percent of nonattenders.

A well-done study by two Dutch sociologists, using many more questions about volunteering and based on data from the World Values Surveys, found very similar results: the percentage who had volunteered was higher in the United States (38.4 percent) than in any Western European nation. They also found that church attendance was a strong predictor of volunteering.[7]

Returning to the United States, a survey conducted in 1999 asked respondents how many hours they had devoted to volunteer work during the past month. Forty-four percent of weekly attenders had devoted no time to volunteer work, compared with 79 percent of the nonattenders; 22 percent of weekly attenders reported putting in three or more hours, compared with 6 percent of nonattenders.[8]

CIVIC PARTICIPATION: BOWLING TOGETHER

Until recently, generations of liberal social critics mourned the demise of American individualism, charging that Americans had become a nation of joiners and conformists. Ralph Waldo Emerson complained that Americans joined organizations in the spirit of "I have failed, and you have failed, but perhaps together we shall not fail."[9] During the 1920s, celebrated novelists such as Sinclair Lewis[10] savagely depicted the conformity of small towns where life was organized on the basis of clubs and lodges, which were said to impose a strict conformity on life and to still independent thought. The 1950s saw the culmination of this critique. First came David Riesman's *The Lonely Crowd*, wherein it was claimed that Americans had become "other-directed," relentless joiners who took all their opinions and tastes from those around them. William Whyte's *The Organization Man* followed, which charged that corporations were stifling individualism. Many similar books and movies appeared, all of them stressing the virtues of individualism.

But then liberal critics did an about-face. In their widely praised *Habits of the Heart* (1985), Robert Bellah and his coauthors condemned individualism and regretted that Americans were not joiners. Instead, they charged, Americans had become even more radically individualistic since earlier times and therefore are unable to understand themselves "as interrelated in morally meaningful ways with" others.[11] If the nation is not to decline into "despotism,"[12] Americans must define themselves "by their relationships and commitments to large wholes."[13] In 2000 this attack on individualism culminated in another academic best-seller: *Bowling Alone*. In this lengthy portrayal of the demise of American community, Harvard's Robert D. Putnam detailed the decline of social and community organizations, from fraternal lodges to bowling leagues, hence the clever title.

Among Putnam's claims was that there had been a long decline in American church attendance and membership, but nothing of the sort has happened. To the contrary, while attendance has held steady, membership has continued to rise. On the other hand, Putnam no doubt was correct that membership in fraternal groups such as the Elks, Eagles, and Masons, as well as service clubs such as Rotary, are in serious decline. That may be true of bowling leagues, too. But does this mean we are becoming a nation of loners (selfish or otherwise), or does it simply reflect a change in which organizations are thriving? That many novels now have a section at the back to help guide book club discussions suggests such clubs have become far more common. In fact, 10 percent of Americans now say they regularly participate in a Bible study group not affiliated with a congregation;[14] this also seems to be something quite new.

And what about bicycle-riding clubs, environmental groups, and fantasy sports leagues? By itself, the enormous popularity of online social networking makes it difficult to accept claims about the rise of American loners.

The 2005 Baylor National Religion Survey asked Americans about their membership in fourteen kinds of voluntary organizations.[15] Dropping "church or other religious organizations" (so as not to contaminate the correlation with church attendance), the results are shown in Tables 6.4 A and B.

TABLE 6.4A. AMERICANS MEMBERSHIP IN VOLUNTARY ORGANIZATIONS (Excludes Church or Religious Organizations)

Organization Type	Percentage Who Belong
Sports, hobby, or leisure club/group	20%
Political party, club, or association	16%
Trade union or professional association	16%
Neighborhood group or association	14%
Other group/organization	12%
School fraternities, sororities, or alumni association	10%
Arts or cultural organization	10%
Internet-based club, group, or chat room	9%
Civic or service group	8%
Youth groups or organizations	5%
Therapeutic or counseling group	4%
Ethnic or racial organization	2%

Source: Baylor National Religious Survey 2007.

To summarize these data, an index of organizational membership was calculated, with the following results:

TABLE 6.4B. INDEX OF ORGANIZATIONAL MEMBERSHIP

No memberships	41%
One to three memberships	48%
Four or more memberships	11%
Total	100%

Source: Baylor National Religious Survey 2007.

About six Americans out of ten belong to at least one voluntary organization. Add in church organizations and the number rises to more than seven out of ten, and the median becomes two memberships.

These findings suggest that Americans may have become less likely to bowl, but not more likely to bowl alone. We remain a nation of joiners. Indeed, Table 6.5 shows how much more likely Americans are than are Western Europeans to be active in a political party.

Notice that these World Values Survey data are in precise

TABLE 6.5. PERCENTAGE ACTIVE IN A POLITICAL PARTY

United States	16%
Switzerland	8%
Netherlands	4%
Norway	4%
Finland	3%
France	3%
Italy	3%
Sweden	3%
United Kingdom	3%
Germany	2%
Spain	1%

Source: World Values Survey 2002–2004.

agreement with the Baylor data on American political party participation. In any event, Americans are twice as likely as the Swiss to be active in a party; four times as likely as the Dutch and the Norwegians; more than five times as likely as the Finns, French, Italians, and the Swedes; eight times as likely as the Germans; and sixteen times as likely as the Spanish.

Finally (not shown), a modest but positive correlation exists between church attendance and organizational membership: 15 percent of weekly attenders belong to four or more organizations, compared with 8 percent of those who never attend.

RELIGION AND POLITICS

Churchgoing Americans (18 percent) are more likely than nonattenders (11 percent) to belong to a political party.[16] Aside from that, no meaningful differences are apparent between attenders and nonattenders on other measures of political activity: voting, being registered, giving money to candidates, or working in campaigns.[17] This would surprise many journalists who have been misled by the concerted efforts to portray Evangelical Protestants as determined to take over the government and destroy democracy.

A survey of a national sample of college and university professors conducted in 2006 found that 53 percent admitted to having negative feelings toward Evangelical Protestants, compared with 3 percent having such feelings toward Jews and 18 percent toward atheists.[18] Fear of Evangelicals is so widespread among academics and most intellectuals partly because of a raft of recent books about evangelical conspiracies—although these books also reflect the prevalence of these fears.

In his best-selling *American Theocracy* (2007) Kevin Phillips identified President George W. Bush as the "theocrat-in-chief," described Evangelicals as the victims of "half-baked preaching," and peppered his book with quotations denouncing Evangelicals, such as Harvey Cox's claim that evangelical religion is a "toxin endangering the health—even the life—of the Christian churches and American society."[19] This earned Phillips fulsome praise in *Time* magazine, the *New York Times*, and other major media outlets. Even so, Phillips was topped by the angry atheist Sam Harris, who claimed, "Tens of millions of our neighbors are working each day to obliterate the separation of church and state, to supplant scientific rationality with Iron Age fantasies, and to achieve a Christian theocracy in the twenty-first century."[20] And Rabbi James Rudin began his revelation of *The Religious Right's Plans for the Rest of Us* as follows: "A specter is haunting America. . . . It is the specter of Americans kneeling in submission to a particular interpretation of religion. . . . It is the specter of a nation ruled by the extreme Christian right, who would make the United States a 'Christian nation' wherein their version of God's law supersedes all human law."[21]

So many books warning against an evangelical takeover have been published that they constitute a separate literary genre— although the number of new titles has been declining in the past several years. Unfortunately, even most of the far more temperate and informed commentators on the politics of evangelical Americans share with the extremists the belief that Evangelicals are very different from other Americans, that they are far more conservative politically, and that their conservatism is rooted in old-fashioned moral convictions on such matters as sexual norms and in right-wing views concerning economic issues such as welfare—but most of all they are extremists in their opposition to the separation of church and state.

Given how often these political and moral issues are included in national surveys, it is amazing that little or no effort has been devoted to documenting these charges against Evangelicals. Perhaps they are regarded as so self-evident as to need no factual substantiation. Or could it be because the facts are quite otherwise?

Identifying Evangelicals

Typically, Evangelical respondents have been identified on the basis of their denominational affiliation. Hence, Baptists, Nazarenes, Pentecostals, and members of other conservative denominations are classified as Evangelicals, while Presbyterians, Episcopalians, and other religious liberals are excluded. This approach is unsatisfactory for two reasons. First, when given the opportunity to identify themselves as "Evangelicals" in the 2007 Baylor National Religion Survey, many members of conservative denominations did not do so. Second, many members of the more liberal denominations, and even some Roman Catholics, did claim to be Evangelicals, as Table 6.6 shows.

TABLE 6.6. WHO IS AN EVANGELICAL?

	Identified Themselves as Evangelicals
Conservative Protestants	49%
Nondenominational Protestants	44%
Liberal Protestants	28%
Roman Catholics	14%
No religion	2%
Total sample	28%

Source: Baylor National Religious Survey 2007.

Obviously, to infer who is and is not an Evangelical from one's denominational affiliation is, at best, a very inaccurate measure and justified only (if ever) when self-identification data are unavailable. Moreover, this is why the proper term is "Evangelical Christian," not "Evangelical Protestant."

Church and State

The principle of the complete separation of church and state is quite new, having first been asserted by the Supreme Court in

1947. Until then, the First Amendment was interpreted quite literally: "Congress shall make no law respecting the establishment of religion or prohibiting the free exercise thereof." That was long taken to mean that the government could not finance a religious group or pass discriminatory laws against religious groups. Period! No one suggested that the government was required to be strictly secular. Abraham Lincoln and his Treasury secretary were entirely aware of the First Amendment when they put "In God we trust" on coins and currency. But then, in 1947, in the case of *Everson v. Board of Education*, the Supreme Court ruled (5-4) that "the First Amendment has erected a wall between church and state. That must be kept high and impregnable. We must not approve the slightest breach."[22]

Subsequently, this ruling has been expanded and reinforced by decisions such as those outlawing school prayers and displays of religious symbols on government property. Out went Christmas nativity scenes on public land; down went the Ten Commandments from schoolroom and courthouse walls. Soon it was illegal for school choirs to sing Christmas carols or for students eating in school cafeterias to say grace out loud.[23]

Evangelical Christians are widely accused of wishing to reverse these rulings, a desire that is frequently offered as evidence of their theocratic aims. These claims are tested in Table 6.7.

If one looked only at the third section of this table, one might agree that Evangelicals pose a threat to the strict separation of church and state; only one-third support it. But that interpretation must change dramatically when one looks at the upper two parts of the table. There we see that while most Evangelicals agree that it ought to be legal to display religious symbols in public places, so does most everyone else. The same is true of school prayer. What seems evident is that Evangelicals are better informed as to what "strict" separation of church and state means—that it prohibits school prayers and public religious displays, among other things. For most Americans, strict separation of church and state would seem to be merely a slogan that

TABLE 6.7. SEPARATION OF CHURCH AND STATE

Do you agree or disagree that the federal government should:

1. *"allow the display of religious symbols in public spaces?"*

	Agree
Evangelicals	88%
Liberal Protestants	72%
Roman Catholics	74%
No Religion	26%
All Non-Evangelicals	61%

2. *"allow prayer in public schools?"*

	Agree
Evangelicals	94%
Liberal Protestants	67%
Roman Catholics	76%
No Religion	21%
All Non-Evangelicals	60%

3. *"enforce a strict separation of church and state?"*

	Agree
Evangelicals	33%
Liberal Protestants	53%
Roman Catholics	54%
No Religion	81%
All Non-Evangelicals	58%

Source: Baylor National Religion Survey 2007.

has the blessing of the media, and they are unaware that it is in contradiction of their specific views.

The most important lesson to be drawn from Table 6.7 is that if a national referendum were held to restore school prayer and to allow such things as nativity scenes on public property, even if Evangelicals were not allowed to vote, the referendum would pass by a landslide. On the other hand, Evangelicals do not fully reject the separation of church and state. When asked whether the federal government should "fund faith-based organizations" (not shown), the overwhelming majority said, "No."

Let us now turn to social and economic issues. Four items seem to provide sufficient coverage. Persons surveyed were asked if the federal government should

- ▶ Regulate business practices more closely.
- ▶ Distribute wealth more evenly.
- ▶ Do more to protect the environment.
- ▶ Spend more on the military.

Responses appear in Table 6.8.

TABLE 6.8. SOCIAL AND ECONOMIC ISSUES

	Regulate Business	Distribute Wealth	Protect Environment	Spend on Military
Evangelicals	60%	46%	76%	55%
Liberal Protestants	64%	52%	82%	51%
Roman Catholics	66%	54%	83%	53%
No Religion	75%	70%	93%	27%
All Non-Evangelicals	66%	59%	84%	47%

Source: Baylor National Religion Survey 2007.

Reading down the columns, the overall finding is that Evangelicals are pretty much like everyone else in terms of their social and economic outlook. Thus, most Americans support closer regulation of business, as do most Evangelicals. A majority of Americans want the government to do more to distribute wealth more evenly, and almost half of Evangelicals agree. The overwhelming majority of Americans want the government to do more to protect the environment, and so do 76 percent of Evangelicals. Americans are about evenly split on increased funding for the military, and so are Evangelicals.

Turning to the so-called moral issues, three major items are revealing, as shown in Table 6.9.

- ▸ The government should abolish the death penalty.
- ▸ The government should promote affirmative-action programs.
- ▸ Abortion is wrong when the only reason is that the woman does not want the child.

TABLE 6.9. MORAL ISSUES

	Abolish Death Penalty	Promote Affirmative Action	Abortion Wrong*
Evangelicals	16%	34%	94%
Liberal Protestants	20%	47%	60%
Roman Catholics	18%	42%	75%
No Religion	34%	47%	24%
All Non-Evangelicals	20%	47%	63%

*When the only reason for the abortion is that the woman does not want the child.

Source: Baylor National Religion Survey 2007.

Here, too, we see that Evangelicals aren't that different when compared to other Americans, as opposed to the positions favored by the media. While only 16 percent of Evangelicals would repeal the death penalty, only 20 percent of non-Evangelicals would do so. The majority of Evangelicals don't want the government promoting affirmative-action programs, but neither do most other Americans. Evangelicals are nearly unanimous in their opposition to an abortion on the grounds offered in the question, but nearly two-thirds of non-Evangelicals agree with them.

Back in the 1940s and 1950s, many popular books and articles in magazines such as *The Nation* exposed the alleged secret plans by the pope and his Catholic minions to take over America and stamp out all traces of democracy. In his 1949 best-seller, *American Freedom and Catholic Power*, Paul Blanshard devoted many pages to details of the theocratic regime the pope had in store for America, if he were not stopped. Blanshard proposed that Protestant Americans organize "a resistance movement to prevent the [Catholic] hierarchy from imposing its social policies upon our schools, hospitals, government and family organizations."[24]

Today these anti-Catholic concerns seem ridiculous. Hopefully, the equally spurious claims about Evangelical theocratic plots will also soon seem ridiculous as well, for the fact is that Evangelicals are not so very different after all.

Conclusion

Churchgoing Americans most closely fulfill Theodore Roosevelt's definition of a good citizen. They pull their weight by their higher levels of generosity with their money and their time. Contrary to common stereotypes fostered by academics and the media, religious Americans have not caused us to become a nation of individualists who prefer to bowl alone. Finally, Evangelical Christians are not the threat to democracy they too often are made out to be. They aren't even very different in their political and moral views from non-Evangelicals.

* 7 *

Achievement and Success

THE GERMAN SOCIOLOGIST Max Weber was long honored for his "discovery" that capitalism was invented by Europeans infused with the "Protestant Ethic."[1] Unfortunately, Weber overlooked the fact that fully developed capitalism had flourished in Europe for many centuries prior to the Reformation.[2] However, simply because Weber's thesis was a historical blunder should not discredit his underlying insight that a significant connection exists between religion and economic achievement. Indeed, capitalism originated in the great Christian monastic estates during the ninth and tenth centuries.[3]

Education also has a long, intimate, and persistent connection to religion. The medieval church invented the university, and the Puritans in New England first established public primary schools dedicated to universal education.

This chapter surveys the extent to which these connections remain intact. Are religious Americans more likely to succeed in school and in their occupational lives? Do these effects include African Americans and Hispanic Americans?

EDUCATION

Chapter 3 showed that the very effective homeschooling movement is based primarily on the desire of religious parents to maximize their children's education. It seems likely that similar concerns would lead religious parents to pay particular attention to their children's performance in school. Indeed, this was an article of faith among the early Puritans of New England. They not only paid close attention to the effectiveness of the local schoolmaster, but they also monitored their children's academic progress at home.[4]

The initial focus of this section is on religion and student achievement. Next I examine the effectiveness of religious schools. Finally, we look at a controversy over the impact of religion on attending college.

Student Achievement

Religious students have a superior level of academic achievement, however it is measured.[5] Compared with less religious students, religious students

- ▸ Score higher on all standardized achievement tests.
- ▸ Get better grades.
- ▸ Are more likely to do their homework.
- ▸ Are less likely to be expelled or suspended.
- ▸ Are less likely to drop out of school.

No one disputes these findings. What is widely disputed it *why* these correlations exist. Some have dismissed them as spurious findings, claiming that they merely reflect that religious students come from higher-income families. However, the religious effect holds within all levels of family income.[6]

Others have tried to attribute the religious effect to neighborhoods—that religious kids tend to come from better neighborhoods. In fact, the religious effect holds in all neighborhoods.[7]

Still others have proposed that these results hold only for white students, but the religious effect on school achievement holds even more strongly for African American and Hispanic students.[8]

However, the seemingly most plausible challenge to the claim that religion influences academic achievement suggests that it is not religion but the family life of religious students that results in their superior performances. Research shows that religious parents have higher expectations for their children's school performance; they more often discuss school with their children, including the content of courses; they encourage their children to take more demanding courses; they require that regular time be set aside for homework; they better supervise their children and otherwise create a home atmosphere conducive to achievement.[9] In addition, religious students have higher expectations about their own school performances, they study more, and they are far less likely to cut classes or skip school.[10]

But these family and individual factors do not explain away the religious influence on academic achievement. They suggest *how* religion has this effect. That is, religion stimulates a very favorable family life and effective student attitudes and behaviors, which in turn support academic achievement.

Moreover, there remains room for an additional direct religious effect on achievement. As Christian Smith put it, "There is something particularly religious in religion, which is not reducible to nonreligious explanations. . . . [Religion directly exerts] pro-social influences in the lives of youth not by happenstance or generic social processes . . . [but] precisely as an outcome of . . . particular theological, moral, and spiritual commitments."[11] A fine body of research supports this view. After controlling for all these family and individual effects, a significant religious effect on academic achievement remains.[12]

Religious Schools

The findings reported above are not based on comparisons between students at religious schools and those in the public schools. The studies were all based on public school students and compared the more religious with the less religious. But when the performance of students at religious schools is compared with those at public schools, the results are dramatic. Students at religious schools perform far better on all measures of achievement. Of course, relentless efforts have been made to dismiss these findings as spurious.

The primary charge is selection bias—that the religious schools only admit the better students. Through the years, quite extraordinary efforts have been made to evaluate this claim, often by researchers who began with the belief that, in fact, selection bias does account for the superior performance of religious school students. But these efforts have failed. Statistical controls for student backgrounds do not eliminate or even substantially reduce the differences between public and religious schools.[13] In fact, even most students with records of poor academic achievement prior to entering a religious school soon show great improvement. As we see below, minority students may benefit the most from attending religious schools.

The reasons that religious schools excel are not all that difficult to discover. They benefit from having far more dedicated teachers (most of them working for much lower salaries), are quite effective at involving parents in their children's educations, and sustain a context far more conducive to learning. Far less cutting of classes and truancy takes place. Perhaps even more important, there is far less misbehavior, such as talking back to teachers, let alone threatening to attack them, both of which often occur in many public schools. There also is greater racial harmony and far less violence at religious schools, as well as far less drug use and delinquency. Finally, faculty at religious schools impose higher standards of performance.[14]

Table 7.1 is based on data from a national survey involving more than fifty thousand students, known as the High School and Beyond Study. The table shows how incredibly more effective the Catholic schools are in graduating their students— especially those from lower-income and minority families. While 28 percent of students from the families in the lowest economic group dropped out of public schools, only 7 percent of students from similar economic backgrounds dropped out of Catholic schools. Similarly, 22 percent of African Americans dropped out of public schools, while only 2 percent dropped out of Catholic schools. For Hispanics, this comparison is 23 percent versus 6 percent.

TABLE 7.1. DROPOUT RATES
(Percentage Dropping Out before Graduating)

	Public Schools	Catholic Schools
Family Economic Status		
Lowest	28%	7%
Lower	16%	2%
Higher	13%	0%
Highest	8%	1%
Race and Ethnic Background		
White	17%	1%
African American	22%	2%
Hispanic	23%	6%

Source: Stark 2007, 461.

The Achievement Gap

Perhaps the most troubling aspect of American education is the great achievement gap between white students and their African American classmates. The gap exists on every measure of achievement: standardized test scores, grades, being held back a grade, and staying in school.[15] By the time he or she enters middle school, the average African American student scores several grade levels behind the average white student of the same age on standardized tests of reading and arithmetic. The differences are even greater by age 17.

Although an achievement gap also exists between whites and Hispanics, it is regarded as primarily the result of so many Hispanics being recent immigrants. Similar gaps once existed for other immigrant groups but quickly disappeared, and educationists seem confident that this scenario will hold true for Hispanics as well. This view is supported by research showing that Hispanic achievement scores not only rise across generations in the United States,[16] but that even for first-generation Hispanic students, the gap narrows as they progress through school.[17]

But, the white–African American educational achievement gap cannot be attributed to recent immigration, and it has responded little to a variety of programs aimed at overcoming it. For example, since a significant gap already exists when students begin school, the Head Start Program was initiated in 1965 to compensate for preschool disadvantages. But studies have found that even if there are any slight positive initial effects of Head Start (and there may well not be any), they quickly disappear after children start school.[18] Of course, heavy federal funding of Head Start continues. The No Child Left Behind program was begun in 2001, aimed at testing and improving the schools with the goal, in part, of reducing the achievement gap. Making schools accountable turned out to be very difficult to accomplish, especially against the vigorous opposition of the teachers' unions. There may have been a small reduction in the white–African American educational achievement gap over the past decade, but a very substantial and damaging gap remains. Still, when it comes to the achievement gap and religious schools,

- ► The achievement gap between whites and African Americans is considerably smaller in religious schools than in the public schools.
- ► The achievement gap is smaller among students who are religious.

▶ The gap also is smaller among students having intact families—who live with both their father and their mother. When William Jeynes[19] combined all three factors, he found that among religious students at religious schools, and among students who come from intact families, there is no academic achievement gap. Under these conditions, African American students do as well as whites, and both groups excel.

As to educational policy, nothing can be done to make more students religious or to increase the number of intact families. But school vouchers would certainly make religious schools accessible to many more lower-income families and might spur effective improvements in public schools.

Going to College

Many people today assume that the epitome of academic achievement is graduating from college. The fact that many graduates are woefully ignorant and even have very limited capacity to read or do simple arithmetic seems little recognized. However, the stereotype remains that religious people tend to be uneducated. This belief is often traced to two studies published by Alfred Darnell and Darren Sherkat.[20] In fact, all that these two sociologists demonstrated was the obvious: that some very small and marginal groups of Christian fundamentalists tend to disdain sending their children to college. But, it is as inappropriate to generalize these findings to "religious Americans" as it would be to claim that all churchgoing American men have beards, based on a study of the Amish. Moreover, when Kraig Beyerlein distinguished groups within the category of Protestant fundamentalists more carefully, he found that Evangelical Protestants were second only to Jews in being college-educated, significantly exceeding all other religious groups as well as the nonreligious.[21]

Given that religious students in general do significantly better in school and on achievement tests, it would be surprising if they were not more likely to attend college. Strangely enough, aside from Beyerlein's study noted above, I was able to find only one solid published study on the educational attainment of church attenders—it reported that the more often students attended church, the more likely they were to enroll in college.[22] To supplement this finding, I used the combined samples of the General Social Surveys to calculate Table 7.2.

TABLE 7.2. CHURCH ATTENDANCE AND EDUCATION

Whites Only			
	Church Attendance		
	Weekly	Sometimes	Never
Attended college	22%	20%	17%
Attended junior college	4%	5%	4%
High school graduate	52%	54%	50%
Less than high school	22%	21%	29%
Total	100%	100%	100%

Significance <.00

African Americans Only			
	Church Attendance		
	Weekly	Sometimes	Never
Attended college	11%	9%	6%
Attended junior college	5%	5%	4%
High school graduate	48%	51%	46%
Less than high school	36%	34%	44%
Total	100%	100%	100%

Significance: <.00

Source: General Social Surveys, combined years.

Reading across the table, among both whites and African Americans, weekly attenders are more likely than those who never attend church to have gone to college and less likely to have not completed high school. Although the differences are not large, they are very significant statistically. The idea that churchgoers tend to be less educated is false.

But what do they do with their educations?

OCCUPATIONAL PRESTIGE

One thing churchgoers are less likely to do with their educations is become college professors—although, ironically, those who do are far more apt to be natural and physical scientists than to pursue the social sciences or the humanities.[23] But the halls of academia do not monopolize the supply of high-prestige occupations. Moreover, occupational prestige is one of the most carefully studied topics in the social sciences.

In 1947 Paul Hatt and Cecil North presented a national sample of American adults with a list of eighty-seven occupational titles.[24] Each respondent was asked to rate the "general standing" of each job as excellent (5), good (4), average (3), somewhat below average (2), or poor (1). From these numerical weights, an average score was computed for each occupation. It was possible for an occupation to score anywhere from 20 to 100. In fact, the highest occupation was "U.S. Supreme Court justice" with a score of 94, and the lowest was "Shoe shiner," which scored 34. These scores were identified as a measure of occupational prestige.

In 1962 this study was repeated, and the results were identical. Subsequently, it was discovered that occupational prestige scores for occupations could be predicted with a very high degree of accuracy on the basis of the average education of persons in that occupation and their average salary. Thus, one could generate occupational prestige ratings for every occupation employing a significant number of people.

Table 7.3 shows that among both whites and African Americans, weekly attenders are more likely than those who never attend to hold an upper-prestige occupation (upper 15 percent) and significantly less likely to hold a lower prestige occupation (bottom third).

TABLE 7.3. RELIGION AND OCCUPATIONAL PRESTIGE

Whites			
	Church Attendance		
	Weekly	Sometimes	Never
Occupational Prestige			
Upper	18%	14%	12%
Middle	54%	54%	51%
Lower	28%	32%	37%
Total	100%	100%	100%

Significance <.00

African Americans			
	Church Attendance		
	Weekly	Sometimes	Never
Occupational Prestige			
Upper	11%	6%	6%
Middle	35%	38%	30%
Lower	54%	56%	64%
Total	100%	100%	100%

Significance: <.00

Source: General Social Surveys, combined years.

Given that religious Americans are more apt to have college degrees, one would expect this result. In fact, when education is held constant, religion has no direct effect on occupational prestige. Some would argue that these results show that religion does not influence occupational achievement. I would disagree. In my judgment, religion influences occupational success through education; by doing better in school, churchgoing Americans end up in better jobs.

WEALTH

Surveys are not well designed to measure wealth. Asking a question about net worth on a survey is futile, because very few people walk around with such a figure in their heads and must devote considerable time and effort to providing an estimate even when filling out a loan application. Asking a respondent's annual income is known to result in quite unreliable data, marred by a high level of refusal to answer. Consequently, I have settled for two rather limited measures that have the virtue of very low refusal rates and being easy to answer accurately: owning a home and investing in the stock market.

Table 7.4 shows that among both whites and African Americans, weekly church attenders are far more likely to own their homes than are those who never attend.

Table 7.5 shows responses to the question, "In the past twelve months have you invested money in a stock or mutual funds?" Weekly attenders are significantly more likely to have done so. The table is limited to whites because there were too few African American respondents to yield reliable results, although 18 percent of weekly attenders had invested in the market, compared with only 9 percent of nonattenders. These results concerning wealth probably can be entirely accounted for by the superior educations and occupations of weekly church attenders. Again, that does not dismiss religious effects, but implicates them in a causal chain that begins with superior school achievement.

TABLE 7.4. RELIGION AND HOME OWNERSHIP

	Whites		
	Church Attendance		
	Weekly	Sometimes	Never
Own their home	75%	63%	56%

	African Americans		
	Church Attendance		
	Weekly	Sometimes	Never
Own their home	51%	37%	31%

Source: General Social Surveys, combined years.

TABLE 7.5. RELIGION AND MARKET INVESTMENTS
(Whites Only)

	Church Attendance			
	Weekly	Sometimes	Never	Significance
Invested in past year	32%	30%	22%	<.00

Source: General Social Surveys 2000; 2002.

Economic Hardship

The flip side of occupational prestige and wealth is economic hardship. One measure of hardship is unemployment, and Table 7.6 shows that weekly attenders are much less likely to ever have been unemployed—a results that holds true for whites and African Americans.

Table 7.7 shows that among whites, those who never attend church are more than twice as likely as weekly attenders to have been behind on their rent or mortgage payments within the

TABLE 7.6. RELIGION AND UNEMPLOYMENT

Whites			
	Church Attendance		
	Weekly	Sometimes	Never	Significance
Ever unemployed	20%	32%	37%	<.00

African Americans			
	Church Attendance		
	Weekly	Sometimes	Never	Significance
Ever unemployed	31%	42%	47%	<.00

Source: General Social Surveys, combined years.

past year (there were insufficient cases to support findings for African Americans). Among both whites and African Americans, those who never attend church are far more likely to have ever been on welfare than have weekly attenders.

The religious effect is not direct, but is channeled through education and occupation. Such indirectness does not make the religious effect less real.

CONCLUSION

Religious Americans achieve high levels of occupational and economic success, but doing well in school isn't the only reason. Considering the previous chapters, religious Americans obviously have many other advantages that play an important role in their careers. They are far less likely to be handicapped by having police records. They are far more likely to display attractive personal characteristics such as niceness and generosity. They are less likely to come from broken homes, and more likely to

TABLE 7.7. RELIGION AND HARDSHIP

Whites			
	Church Attendance		
	Weekly	Sometimes	Never	Significance
Behind on rent or mortgage in past year*	4%	9%	11%	<.00
Has ever been on welfare**	28%	37%	43%	<.00

African Americans			
	Church Attendance		
	Weekly	Sometimes	Never	Significance
Has ever been on welfare**	37%	50%	55%	<.00

Source: *General Social Survey 1991; **General Social Surveys, combined years.

have been raised to develop self-discipline and responsibility. They are far less prone to messy and expensive divorces, to premarital pregnancies, and extramarital scandals. They are less subject to depression and neurosis, both of which can devastate careers. They are healthier, hence less subject to absenteeism, and probably they are more energetic. They are more sociable and more apt to have and to form career-advancing relationships. In short, religiousness is not merely a matter of private belief or of spending an hour every week sitting in a pew. It is a comprehensive lifestyle that involves participation in extended social networks.

* 8 *

Intellectual Life

THE HIGHLY RESPECTED Christian scholar Mark A. Noll began one of his best-known books with this sentence: "The scandal of the evangelical mind is that there is not much of an evangelical mind." In the next paragraph Noll charged that the churches "have nourished millions of believers in the simple verities of the gospel but have largely abandoned . . . the arts, and other realms of high culture."[1]

Noll was not expressing an original thought. Rather, his conclusions were the culmination of a long series of claims made during the twentieth century that religion is incompatible with the life of the mind. Indeed, in 1964 Richard Hofstadter won the Pulitzer Prize for *Anti-Intellectualism in American Life* (1962), in which he argued that a preference for ignorance is inherent in American Christianity.[2] Little wonder, then, that media types so often express contempt for religious people, or that, when speaking to an elite group of San Francisco donors, then–presidential candidate Barack Obama disdained middle Americans as those who "cling to guns or religion."

But is it true? Are religious Americans really a bunch of anti-intellectual, credulous philistines?

For most of this chapter I don't cite research literature, because there is none. Although appropriate data are available, no one has bothered to use them for these purposes. I make considerable use of the excellent Arts and Religion Survey designed by the distinguished Robert Wuthnow.[3] These data are invaluable for testing notions about religiousness and high culture, but that was not why Wuthnow conducted his study. He was interested in how the arts influence religion, not in testing notions about the lack of culture among religious people.

HIGH CULTURE

It is an article of faith in sophisticated circles that, aside from a small set of intellectuals (mainly living in New York and Boston), Americans are sadly lacking in culture, and this is taken to be doubly so for religious Americans. Let Richard Hofstadter explain why:

> One begins with the hardly contestable proposition that religious faith is not, in the main, propagated by logic and learning. One moves on from this to the idea that it is best propagated . . . by men who have been unlearned and ignorant. It seems to follow from this that the kind of wisdom and truth possessed by such men is superior to what learned and cultivated minds have. . . . Accordingly, though one shrinks from a bald statement of the conclusion, humble ignorance is far better as a human quality than a cultivated mind. At bottom, this proposition . . . has been eminently congenial both to American evangelicalism and to American democracy.[4]

Reading

Possibly the most essential feature of the life of the mind is reading. Several of my former publishers told me that Christians don't read. When I asked how they knew, they looked at me askance; wasn't it obvious? When I persisted, one said that

Christian bookstores don't stock many books. True enough, and what they do stock are mainly devotional books, but it is not clear that they really are bookstores despite their name; "bookstore" is a more dignified name than "Christian merchandise mart." In any event, how these stores are stocked tells us nothing about Christian reading habits. However, Tables 8.1 and 8.2 do.

The tables include only white respondents because substantial racial differences reduce the religion effect; African Americans are overrepresented in the weekly attender group. For the most part, the same correlations hold among African Americans as among whites, but they often fall short of statistical significance because they are based on so few cases—there being only 209 African Americans in the Arts and Religion Survey, for example, only 18 of whom never attend church.

TABLE 8.1. HOURS PER DAY SPENT READING (WHITES ONLY)

	Church Attendance			
	Weekly	Sometimes	Never	Significance
More than 2 hours	27%	20%	19%	<.00
1–2 hours	71%	77%	71%	
No hours	2%	3%	10%	
	100%	100%	100%	

Source: Arts and Religion Survey 1999.

Table 8.1 shows that weekly church attenders spend more hours reading than do those who attend less often or never. More than a fourth of weekly attenders devote two or more hours a day to reading, compared with 19 percent of those who never attend. Only 2 percent of weekly attenders do not read, compared with 10 percent of those who never go to church. Because these differences are not huge, I have added the level of significance which is beyond the .oo level, meaning that there is less than one chance in a hundred that these differences are not real, but merely random.

Table 8.2 is devoted to the content of reading. Weekly attenders are far more likely than those who never attend to read a newspaper every day and to have read poetry in the past year. The latter finding reminded me that when I conducted a national survey many years ago, and included a brief set of items asking respondents to identify various people as to being associated with politics, entertainment, sports, or literature, frequent church attenders were far more likely than others to correctly identify the poet Robert Frost.

TABLE 8.2. READING MATTER (WHITES ONLY)

| | Church Attendance | | | |
	Weekly	Sometimes	Never	Significance
Reads a newspaper daily*	49%	46%	35%	<.00
Read poetry this year**	37%	27%	24%	<.00
Reads fiction*	78%	73%	70%	<.05
Read a novel this year**	53%	50%	45%	<.00
Admires writers**	89%	85%	79%	<.00

Source: *General Social Survey 2002. **Arts and Religion Survey 1999.

Table 8.2 also shows that church attenders are more likely to read fiction and to have read a novel in the past year. For the

comparison on reading fiction, the significance level of beyond
.05 means there is less than one chance in twenty that these
differences are random and not real. Finally, everyone admires
writers, but weekly attenders are significantly more likely to
admire them than are nonattenders.

Obviously, my former publishers were wrong. Christians
read. Indeed, how else to explain the existence of a number of
very profitable Christian publishing houses? Indeed, how else
to explain why my former publishers gave me substantial cash
advances for books that appealed primarily to Christians, as is
attested by the many emails I receive from readers?

Music and Arts

One can be an avid reader and still be a lowbrow anti-
intellectual. Indeed, Hofstadter buttressed his case for American
anti-intellectualism by noting contemptuously that President
Dwight Eisenhower read western novels, in contrast with his
defeated opponent Adlai Stevenson, who was believed to have
high-culture tastes.[5] So, what about religion and high culture?

Surely, classical music is an appropriate measure. Table 8.3
shows that religious Americans are substantially more likely to
say they like classical music than are nonattenders. Moreover,
weekly attenders are significantly more likely than nonattenders
to have attended a classical music concert or an opera in the
past year. In contrast, weekly attenders are far less apt to say
they like "contemporary" music—which is, of course, rock and
roll; whatever descriptive terms one might apply to rock and
roll, "high culture" would not be among them. Finally, weekly
church attenders are more likely than nonattenders to have
gone to see a stage play in the past year.

The Arts and Religion Survey also asked respondents, "If
we think of the arts as including painting, music of all kinds,
dance, theater, and creative literature, how important would

TABLE 8.3. MUSIC AND THEATER
(WHITES ONLY)

	Church Attendance			
	Weekly	Sometimes	Never	Significance
Likes classical music*	53%	44%	37%	<.00
Has attended a classical music or opera performance in the past year (not including school performances)*	23%	18%	17%	<.00
Has attended a live performance of a nonmusical stage play (not including school performances)**	31%	27%	23%	<.00
Especially likes contemporary music***	42%	63%	67%	<.00

Source: *General Social Survey 2002. **General Social Surveys 1998; 2002.
***Arts and Religion Survey 1999.

you say the arts are in your life?" Table 8.4 shows that here, too, weekly attenders place more importance on high culture than do nonattenders.

So much for Noll's claim that the churches have caused Christians to "abandon" the arts. As for claims such as Hofstadter's, they always should have been recognized as left-wing nonsense.

I have not controlled for education or any other factor (aside from race) that might be the real cause of these religious effects. Although many have claimed that religion causes people to be lacking in cultural tastes, I do not propose that religion causes people to have high cultural tastes. My claim is merely descriptive—that religious people are readers and fans of classical music and the arts. Why they have such tastes is beside the point.

TABLE 8.4. THE IMPORTANCE OF THE ARTS IN YOUR LIFE
(WHITES ONLY)

	Church Attendance			
	Weekly	Sometimes	Never	Significance
Very important	49%	43%	42%	<.00
Fairly important	35%	38%	34%	<.00
Not important	16%	19%	24%	<.00
Total	100%	100%	100%	<.00

Source: Arts and Religion Survey 1999.

RELIGIOUS INTELLECTUALISM

Of course, the life of the mind is not exclusively secular. Some of the most impressive intellectuals who ever lived were theologians. It seems likely to me that active Christians also express their intellectualism in religious matters—in what they read and discuss. Fortunately, the Arts and Religion Survey asked four questions that measure aspects of religious intellectualism:

1. How much interest do you have in learning more about religious history?
2. Would you say you are very interested in learning more about other world religions?
3. In school or on your own, how much reading have you done about the history of religion in the United States?
4. How much interest do you have in learning more about religious art?

Table 8.5 shows how these items are related to church attendance.

No doubt these responses are somewhat inflated by knowing that one is supposed to be interested in these matters. Nonetheless, weekly church attenders display far higher levels of interest in these intellectual pursuits—so much so that there is no need to show significance levels.

TABLE 8.5. RELIGIOUS INTELLECTUALISM

	Church Attendance		
	Weekly	Sometimes	Never
Interested in religious history	79%	60%	42%
Interested in world religions	55%	43%	30%
Has read about U.S. religion	47%	30%	29%
Interested in religious art	41%	34%	20%

Source: Arts and Religion Survey 1999.

FAITH AND CREDULITY

A major thrust of the militant attacks on Christianity by the so-called new atheists is credulity. Christians are characterized as childishly immature believers in obvious fantasies such as the existence of God. Yet many of these same folks, including Richard Dawkins and Carl Sagan, have expressed their belief in the probable existence of "godlike" creatures on distant planets, albeit these super races are said to have evolved in an entirely natural manner. In any event, just as with charges that religious Americans disparage high culture, the charge of credulity also is susceptible to empirical investigation.

Bigfoot and Aliens

Some years ago, William Sims Bainbridge and I provoked consternation among the readers of a humanist-sponsored magazine by reporting that in a large sample of college students, those who said they were irreligious were the ones most likely to embrace a series of occult and paranormal beliefs.[6] On the other hand, students who said they had been "born again" and that their religious beliefs were "very important" to them were by far those least likely to accept these beliefs.[7]

Out of respect for these irreligious readers, we refrained from quoting the famous Chesterton quip that when people stop believing in God they are ready to believe anything. Still, scores of readers of the *Skeptical Inquirer* wrote angry letters to the editor and directly to us to assert that such a finding could not possibly be true. But it was. For example, the irreligious were almost three times as likely as were the most religious students to place "great value" in "Tarot readings, séances, and psychic healing." Two-thirds of the irreligious agreed that "UFOs are probably real spaceships from other worlds," compared with 40 percent of the most religious students. We concluded our essay, "Those who hope that a decline in traditional religion would inaugurate a new Age of Reason ought to think again."

Opponents of these results made much of the fact that they were based on 1,439 undergraduates at the University of Washington and therefore the results probably (or most certainly) were peculiar to that institution or area. Moreover, many critics noted that, given a student sample, it was impossible to examine correlations between education and paranormal beliefs, and surely these would show "enlightened" effects. Subsequently, several studies explored educational effects on various paranormal beliefs, but with very mixed results.[8] These same studies also had mixed results as to the correlation between religiousness and paranormal beliefs, but all of these studies were based on nonsamples or were deficient in other ways.

Consequently, the first Baylor National Religious Survey, conducted in 2005, included a set of appropriate questions, selected by my former student and colleague Christopher Bader.[9] Table 8.6 shows the responses, ordered on the basis of the percent who agreed.

There is substantial belief in all nine of these items. Only a minority of Americans disagree with the first five items, a bare

TABLE 8.6 BELIEF IN OCCULT AND PARANORMAL ACTIVITY

Dreams sometimes foretell the future or reveal hidden truths.

Agree	53%
Undecided	17%
Disagree	30%

Ancient advanced civilizations, such as Atlantis, once existed.

Agree	43%
Undecided	30%
Disagree	27%

Places can be haunted.

Agree	37%
Undecided	16%
Disagree	47%

It is possible to influence the physical world through mind alone.

Agree	29%
Undecided	22%
Disagree	49%

Some UFOs are probably spaceships from other worlds.

Agree	24%
Undecided	22%
Disagree	49%

It is possible to communicate with the dead.

Agree	18%
Undecided	19%
Disagree	63%

Creatures such as Bigfoot and the Loch Ness Monster will one day be discovered by science.

Agree	17%
Undecided	27%
Disagree	56%

Astrology impacts one's life and personality.

Agree	14%
Undecided	15%
Disagree	71%

Astrologers, palm readers, tarot-card readers, fortune tellers, and psychics can foresee the future.

Agree	12%
Undecided	15%
Disagree	73%

Source: Baylor National Religion Survey 2005.

majority reject Bigfoot and the Loch Ness Monster, and the astrology items garner the least support.

For purposes of analysis, responses to these nine items were summed to create an Index of Occult and Paranormal Belief. The scores were then separated into quartiles; cutting points were selected that put about 25 percent of the respondents into each of four categories: Low, Medium, Medium High, and High. Many factors were examined as to their influence on belief in the occult and paranormal:

▶ Race: African Americans (41 percent scored high) were far more likely than whites (26 percent) to believe. Consequently, all of the results below are for *whites only*.

▶ Gender: Women (33 percent) are substantially more likely than men (18 percent) to believe.

▶ Age: Of all age groups, those under 30 (41 percent) were the most likely to score high, while those over 60 (16 percent) were least likely. No variations occurred among the other age groups.

▶ Marital status: Unmarried people living together (43 percent) and those who had never married (39 percent) were most likely to believe, while married people (23 percent) and the widowed (21 percent) were least likely.

▶ Region: Geographical differences were modest, but those living in the eastern United States (31 percent) were a bit more likely to score high than people living elsewhere.

▶ Politics: Party preference matters a lot: Only 15 percent of "strong" Republicans scored high versus 38 percent of "strong" Democrats; 18 percent of those who voted for George W. Bush in 2004 scored high, compared with 33 percent of those who voted for John Kerry, and 55 percent of those who voted for Ralph Nader.

▶ Education: Amazingly, education has no significant effect: 26 percent of those who had only finished high school (or less) scored high, compared with 23 percent of those with postgraduate educations.

Now for religion. Table 8.7 shows that people who never attend church are more than twice as likely (30 percent) to score high as are weekly church attenders (14 percent). Conversely, weekly attenders are substantially more likely to score low (35 percent) than are nonattenders (20 percent).

TABLE 8.7. CHURCH ATTENDANCE AND OCCULT AND PARANORMAL BELIEFS (WHITES ONLY)

	Church Attendance		
	Weekly	Sometimes	Never
Occult and Paranormal Index			
High	14%	35%	30%
Medium High	20%	22%	29%
Medium	31%	28%	21%
Low	35%	15%	20%
Total	100%	100%	100%

Source: Baylor National Religion Survey 2005.

Within the churchgoing community there also were marked effects: 12 percent of those who identified themselves as theological conservatives scored high, compared with 40 percent of those who identified themselves as theological liberals. Ten percent of Baptists scored high, compared with 38 percent of Episcopalians.

The findings are clear and strong. Traditional Christian religion greatly decreases credulity as measured by belief in the occult and the paranormal. In contrast, education has no effect. For those concerned about shielding young people from the prevalent occult and paranormal beliefs in our society, it would seem unavailing to send them to college, but quite effective to have them attend a conservative Sunday school.

New Age

Parallel to the decline of belief in basic Christian tenets in liberal Protestant circles, including belief in a conscious God (as outlined in chapter 1), there has arisen a rather vague, very eclectic, and little-organized form of spirituality that has come to be identified as the New Age movement. Often this movement is said to have originated in the 1960s, but that is only when the term "new age" came into popular use. The movement itself dates back to the late nineteenth century, being an amalgam of the mystical teachings of fringe figures such as Emanuel Swedenborg and Helena Blavatsky (founder of theosophy). In 1912 the great German sociologist Ernst Troeltsch was fully aware of this new spirituality, describing it as "mystical . . . nonhistorical, formless, and purely individualistic. . . . Whatever organized forms it does adopt are loose and provisional. . . . In itself, this kind of spirituality feels no need for sacraments. . . . This religious romanticism . . . is the secret religion of the educated classes."[10]

So it has remained. Recently, New Age was described as an elite spiritual movement "drawing on both Eastern and Western spiritual and metaphysical traditions and then infusing them with influences from self-help and motivational psychology, holistic health, parapsychology, [and] consciousness research."[11] In the 1960s, New Age spirituality gained a great deal of national attention through the involvement of many prominent people in the Esalen Institute in Big Sur, California.[12]

The Baylor National Religious Survey of 2005 included items appropriate for measuring involvement in the New Age movement.

> Perhaps nothing so identifies New Agers as their self-identification as seekers. Please indicate the *one* term that best describes your religious identity:
> Seeker   4%

Among the thirteen terms offered, including "Born-Again" and "Evangelical," was "Seeker," and 4 percent of Americans selected it.

Another feature of New Age identity is generic mysticism. These two items seem appropriate measures:

Have you ever had an experience where you felt that . . .

| you were one with the universe? | 19 percent responded "yes." |
| you left your body for a period of time? | 15 percent responded "yes." |

Summing these three items creates a New Age Orientation Index, ranging from 0 through 3. Altogether, 72 percent of Americans scored 0, having rejected all three items. Twenty percent scored 1, 7 percent scored 2, and 1 percent scored 3, having accepted all three items. To facilitate analysis, those scored 2 and 3 were classified as High, scores of 1 were identified as Medium, and those scored 0 were identified as Low.

Table 8.8 demonstrates the validity of this index for measuring New Age orientation.

While only 4 percent of those scored Low on the index have ever visited a New Age bookstore, almost half (47 percent) of those scored High have done so. By the same token, only 3 percent of those scored Low have ever made a purchase at a New Age bookstore, while 38 percent of those scored High have done so. Half of those scored High believe that astrologers, psychics, and palm readers "really" can foresee the future. Three-fourths of those scored High have an interest in yoga, compared with 15 percent of those scored Low. Those scored High (24 percent) are six times as likely as those scored Low (4 percent) to have read *The Celestine Prophecy,* a best-selling New Age novel. And half (51 percent) of High scorers think of God as a somewhat

TABLE 8.8. VALIDATING THE NEW AGE ORIENTATION INDEX

	New Age Index			
	Low	Medium	High	All
Has visited a New Age bookstore	4%	16%	47%	10%
Has made a purchase in a New Age bookstore	2%	12%	38%	7%
Believes that astrologers, psychics, and palm readers "really have the power to foresee the future"	16%	28%	50%	21%
Has an interest in yoga	15%	41%	76%	25%
Has read The Celestine Prophecy	4%	9%	24%	7%
Conceives of God as "a higher power or cosmic force"	8%	19%	51%	14%

Source: Baylor National Survey of Religion 2005.

vague "higher power or cosmic force," compared with 8 percent of Low scorers. Clearly, the index measures what it is supposed to measure: New Age orientation.

Who are the New Agers?

- ▸ There is a small racial difference: 7 percent of whites and 11 percent of African Americans scored High.
- ▸ Perhaps surprisingly, there is no significant gender difference.
- ▸ People under thirty (10 percent) are more likely than are those over sixty (5 percent) to score High, but there are no other significant age differences.

- ► There are no significant regional differences.
- ► "Strong" Democrats (10 percent) are more likely to score high than are "strong" Republicans (2 percent).
- ► Troeltsch was right: New Age is a religion of the educated. Those with postgraduate educations (12 percent) are three times as likely to score High as are those with only high school educations or less (4 percent), while people who attended college (8 percent) fall in between.
- ► People who never attend church (14 percent) are more likely than those who attend sometimes (8 percent) or weekly (4 percent) to score High. Within the churchgoing community there also are very substantial differences. Of those who described themselves as "theologically liberal," 19 percent scored High, in contrast with 2 percent of those who said they were "theologically conservative." Forty percent of Unitarians scored High, as did 82 percent of the Buddhists, and 17 percent of the Jews,[13] as compared with 4 percent of Evangelical Protestants and 5 percent of Roman Catholics. Finally, 16 percent of those who said they had no religion scored High.

CONCLUSION

Clearly, the real scandal involving the "Evangelical mind" is the widespread belief that active Christians are a bunch of uncultured, credulous ignoramuses. But it is not churchgoers who are prone to patronize astrologers or believe in Bigfoot and ghosts. On the other hand, it is church-goers who are most likely to read, to patronize the arts, and to enjoy classical music.

Conclusion: Counting Our Blessings

ONE CAN'T PUT a price tag on happiness, courtesy, nice-ness, or even marital satisfaction. Nor is it possible to convert the suffering caused by crime or ill health into dollar amounts. Even so, it is both possible and appropriate to cal-culate the immense financial sums involved in many of the religious effects demonstrated in the preceding chapters, and that is precisely how I conclude this book. What would it cost if America suddenly were transformed into a fully secularized society? That is, what are the financial implications of assuming that all Americans adopted the patterns set by nonattenders?

It turns out that estimates of costs of the matters in question are easily available from reputable sources, leaving me only with the task of calculating the proportionate changes if the religious effect were removed. While that sometimes required use of rough measures, such enormous sums are involved that errors of a few billion dollars one way or the other seem of little signifi-cance. Readers may wonder why some costs have been omitted, such as the costs to society involved in divorce. These costs are included under other headings, such as welfare (divorce causes some women and children to go on welfare).

CRIME

A huge literature on the costs of crime is available, but many of these studies are incomplete. Some calculate only the costs to crime victims and do not consider costs of the criminal justice system (police, courts, prisons).[1] Even with these omissions, the cost estimates run to hundreds of billions. After carefully surveying the literature, I decided to work with the comprehensive estimate made by David Anderson,[2] which amounted to $1.7 trillion in 1997 dollars ($2.4 trillion in 2011 dollars).

Now, suppose all Americans became irreligious. How much would the costs of crime increase? As reported in Table 2.2, 11 percent of all Americans admitted they had been picked up by the police, compared with 21 percent of those who never attend church. If all Americans were picked up as often as nonattenders, that would be an increase of 91 percent. Assuming that being picked up is a crude but valid measure of the effect of religion on the commission of crimes, then the total secularization of America might well nearly double the costs of crime. Current savings for being a religious society are estimated at $2.1 trillion.

Current savings: **$2.1 trillion.**

HOME AND RELIGIOUS SCHOOLING

Currently, 1.3 million students are being homeschooled, another 2 million are enrolled in Catholic schools, and 3 million in Protestant and Jewish schools—a total of 6.3 million students. What if all these students showed up at the doors of the public schools next fall? Making the conservative assumption that costs per student did not increase in response to this sudden increase in demand, and given that at present the annual cost per public school student exceeds $10,000, a total of $630 million would be added to government spending.

Current savings: **$630 million.**

While we're at it, the Head Start Program can be eliminated since it achieves nothing. This would be a savings of more than $8 billion a year, counting only federal funds. If that money were spent on school vouchers, significant effects on the achievement gap could be achieved.

MENTAL HEALTH

The National Institute of Mental Health, a federal agency, estimates the direct and indirect costs of mental illness at approximately $300 billion. It is very difficult to find a solid basis for assessing the extent to which religiousness is holding down these costs. But a rough metric can be based on Table 5.2. If everyone scored high on the psychic inadequacy scale at the same percentage as nonattenders, that would be an increase of 77 percent. Similarly, the percent of Americans scoring high on neurotic distrust would rise 67 percent. Splitting the difference (72 percent) gives a very rough estimate that should all American become nonattenders, mental health costs could increase by as much as $216 billion.

Current savings: **$216 billion.**

PHYSICAL HEALTH

According to the Office of the Actuary of the Centers for Medicare and Medical Services, in 2009 total American spending on health care by government, insurance companies, employers, and individuals amounted to $2.5 trillion. Obviously this amount would increase were all Americans to become nonattenders, since evidence is abundant that churchgoers are considerably healthier than nonattenders. However, estimating the amount of increase that such a change would involve is difficult. The only general metric available is the difference in life expectancy between weekly attenders and nonattenders. Were average life expectancy to fall to the level of those who never attend church, that would be a decline of 7 percent. Applied to total health-care spending, that would mean a current savings of $175 billion. There is a problem here, however. Weekly attenders are healthier than nonattenders and should, therefore, require substantially less in the way of medical costs. But this might be somewhat offset by the fact that by living longer, weekly attenders have more years of being elderly, a time when medical costs rise. To accurately calculate the net effect of religiousness on medical costs would require many statistics unavailable to me and a very elaborate analysis. Instead, I arbitrarily reduce the $175 billion above by one-third, for a final estimate of $115.5 billion.

Current savings: **$115.5 billion.**

CHARITABLE CONTRIBUTIONS

According to the National Philanthropic Trust, individual Americans donated $211 billion to charities in 2010. Of this amount, $74 billion went to religious organization and $137 billion went to secular causes. Based on Table 6.2, if no one were religious, the percentage of Americans giving to secular charities would fall from 78 percent to 60 percent, or by 23 percent. Hence, approximately $31 billion less would be given.

Current savings: **$31 billion.**

VOLUNTEERING

The Corporation for National and Community Service, a federal agency, estimated that, in 2009, Americans put in 8.1 billion hours of volunteer service. An hourly rate for this service was calculated for each state, based on prevailing wages. The result was an estimate that these volunteer services were worth $169 billion. Based on Table 6.3, if no one went to church, the rate of volunteering for the population as a whole would decline from the present 43 percent to 31 percent, a drop of 28 percent, which would decrease the value of American volunteerism by $47.3 billion.

Current savings: **$47.3 billion.**

UNEMPLOYMENT

According to the U.S. Department of Labor, unemployment payments by both the federal and state governments run to about $100 billion a year. In addition, the real costs of unemployment should include lost wages and benefits, but I have not been able to find such a calculation. Settling for the costs of unemployment payments alone, the data on which Table 7.6 is based show that 30 percent of Americans have been unemployed at some time, while 38 percent of nonattenders have been unemployed. All Americans having the same unemployment rates as nonattenders would involve an increase in those unemployed at some time of 27 percent. Applied to current government costs, America's religiousness yields a savings of $27 billion.

Current savings: **$27 billion**

WELFARE

According to the Government Accounting Office, combined federal and state expenditures on welfare programs totaled $647 billion in 2010. The data on which Table 7.7 is based show that 36 percent of all Americans have ever been on welfare, compared with 43 percent of those who never attend church. If everyone were as apt to be unemployed as are nonattenders, welfare costs would increase by 19 percent; hence, current savings amount to $123 billion.

Current savings: **$123 billion.**

Thus, the total current savings to U.S. society from America's religiousness is $2,660,430,000,000—that is, $2.67 trillion per year.

Whatever else can be said about American religion, it provides a great many tangible benefits to all of us—having an annual cash value of more than $2.6 trillion.

Conclusion

The longshoreman philosopher Eric Hoffer correctly noted, "The hardest arithmetic to master is that which enables us to count our blessings." In that spirit I must admit in conclusion that the calculations offered in this chapter are not merely inadequate, but rather beside the point. Even if individual religiousness contributes more than $2.6 trillion in savings to the United States every year, I suggest that the intangible blessings on American life provided by our unusually high level of religiousness are worth far more. For example, no matter what a rape that did not occur saves us in unspent medical, police, prosecution, and prison costs, it shrinks to triviality when compared with the horror and suffering spared to a woman. I have not even tried to estimate the costs to society of the educational achievement gap afflicting African American students, but whatever it amounts to, that sum is insignificant compared with the life disadvantages suffered by kids who could have gained an adequate education, but did not. And it would surely be disgusting to try to place a cash value on happy marital sex lives, but just as surely they are of immense value. Finally, that someone reads newspapers and books is nice indeed.

Notes

INTRODUCTION
1. Based on the Baylor Survey of American Religion 2007.
2. Allan 2010.
3. February 1, 1993, A10.
4. Schwadel 2011.
5. Marshall, Gilbert, and Ahmanson 2009.
6. Lichter, Rothman, and Lichter 1986, 21–22.
7. Ibid., 21.

CHAPTER 1
1. Finke and Stark 1992.
2. Perry Miller 1939, 35.
3. D. S. Smith 1985.
4. Stark 2011, chapter 15.
5. Gaustad 1987, 15.
6. Whitefield, [1756] 1969, 387.
7. Finke and Stark 1992, 27.
8. A. Smith, [1776] 1981, 2:788–89.
9. Finke and Stark 1992; Stark 2008.
10. Grund in Powell 1967, 77, 80.
11. Quoted in Handlin 1949, 261.
12. Berger 1969, 133–34.
13. Interview in *Christian Century*, October 29, 1997, 972–78.
14. C. Smith 1998, 106.
15. Neitz 1987, 257–58.
16. Davidman 1991 204.

17. Arts and Religion Survey, conducted by the Gallup Organization and available online from the American Religion Data Archive.
18. Berger 1969, 145.
19. Ibid., 146.
20. Wilson 1966, 166.
21. Burdick 1993, 8.
22. Kelley 1972, 2.
23. Bangs 1972.
24. Perry 1973 198.
25. Marty 1976, 71.
26. Stark 2008.
27. Bibby and Brinkerhoff 1973 1983.
28. Hoge and Roozen 1979; Roof and McKinney 1987.
29. Egerton 1974; Shibley 1991.
30. Perrin, Kennedy, and Miller 1997.
31. Paul Miller 1978, 257.
32. Dorrien 2001, xiii.
33. Ahlstrom 1967, 208.
34. Hocking 1912, 249.
35. Ibid., 330.
36. Ibid., 324.
37. Edwards 1965; Rowe 1962.
38. Tillich, [1957] 2009, 10–11.
39. Tillich 1952, 185.
40. Tillich 1951, 236.

41. Ibid., 205.
42. Ibid., 235.
43. Ibid., 239.
44. Edwards 1965; Hammond 1964; Rowe 1962; Wainwright 1971.
45. Stark et al. 1971.
46. Stark and Finke 2000, 261.
47. *The World Tomorrow*, May 10, 1934.
48. Ahlstrom 1972, 803.
49. *Annual Report of the Federal Council of Churches* 1930, 64.
50. *Christian Century*, June 26, 1940, 814–16.
51. Quoted in Woodward 1993, 47.
52. See Ebaugh 1993.
53. Stark and Finke 2000.
54. Danzger 1989; Heilman 2006; Wertheimer 1993.
55. Wertheimer 1993.
56. All of this is based on Baylor National Surveys of Religion and is reported in Stark 2008.
57. March 17, 2009.
58. April 13, 2009.
59. Hout and Fischer 2002; Stark 2004, 125; 2008, 141–46.
60. Stark 2008, 125–31.
61. Stark and Introvigne 2003.
62. Stark 2011.
63. Berger, Davie, and Fokas 2008, 16.
64. Schmied 1996.
65. Beckford 1985, 286.
66. Lodberg 1989.
67. Selthoffer 1997.
68. Grim and Finke 2006.
69. *Ude og Hjemme* 24 (2005).
70. Alvarez 2003.
71. Rydenfelt 1985.
72. In Pettersson 1990, 23.
73. Asberg 1990, 18.
74. Stark and Iannaccone 1994.

CHAPTER 2

1. Johnson and Jang 2012.
2. Cullen 2010, 151.
3. Stark 1992.
4. Calculated by the Violence Policy Center, Washington, DC.
5. Grasmick, Kinsey, and Cochrane 1991; Evans et al. 1995.
6. Stark 1988; 1993.
7. Hindelang, Hirschi, and Weis 1981.
8. Keeping in mind that many of the chronic offenders were in jail and not available to survey interviewers and habitual offenders not in jail at the time would probably not have been sampled, lacking a current address.
9. Hirschi 1969.
10. Hirschi and Stark 1969.
11. Burkett and White 1974.
12. Higgins and Albrecht 1977; Albrecht, Chadwick, and Alcorn 1977.
13. Stark and Bainbridge 1985, chapter 4.
14. Stark, Kent, and Doyle 1982.
15. Stark 1996.
16. Bainbridge and Stark 1981a; 1981b.
17. Data from American Religion Data Archive.com
18. Stark and Glock 1968; Stark 2008.
19. Regnerus 2003a.
20. Stark, Doyle, and Kent 1980; Stark et al. 1983; Stark and Bainbridge 1996.
21. Stark 1984.
22. Kerley, Matthews, and Blanchard 2005.
23. Johnson 2011.

24. Piliavin and Charng 1990.
25. Perrin 2000.
26. Bloodgood, Turnley, and Mudrack 2008.
27. Morgan 1983.
28. Brennan and London 2001.
29. Wallace and Forman 1998.
30. Tittle and Welch 1983.
31. Grasmick, Kinsey, and Cochran 1991.
32. Muller and Ellison 2001.

CHAPTER 3

1. See Goldman 2011.
2. Both quoted in Stark 2007, 527.
3. Myers 2004a.
4. Myers 2004b.
5. Myers 2004a.
6. McAfee 2008.
7. Frejka and Westoff 2008.
8. Women attend church at a higher rate than do men.
9. Gordon and Horowitz 1996.
10. Kluegel 1980; Sherkat and Wilson 1995.
11. People who have not married by then seldom marry, and widowhood is not yet very significant.
12. Ellison and Anderson 2001; Wilcox 2004.
13. Ellison and Anderson 2001.
14. Hirschman and Butler 1981.
15. Landis 1960; Johnson 1973.
16. Pearce and Axinn 1998.
17. Wilcox 1998.
18. Bartkowski and Xu 2000.
19. Wilcox 2002.
20. King 2003, 393.
21. Regnerus 2003b.
22. Smith 2003, 416.
23. For a supportive summary, see Straus 1994.
24. Greven 1990; Capps 1992; 1995.
25. See Ellison 1996, 5.

26. Capps 1992. Capps held an endowed chair in pastoral theology at Princeton Theological Seminary.
27. For a summary, see Ellison 1996.
28. Bartkowski and Wilcox 2000.
29. Rudner 1999.

CHAPTER 4

1. Haught 1997, 24.
2. Lawrence 1985, 33.
3. Reeves 1996, 21.
4. Russell 1970, 287–88.
5. Godbeer 2002, 59; Morgan 1942, 593; Smith 1954, 11.
6. Foster 1999, 727.
7. Ibid., 736.
8. Ibid., 740.
9. Ibid., 741.
10. Ibid., 742.
11. Godbeer 2002, 60.
12. Lane 2000, 381.
13. In ibid.
14. D'Emilio and Freedman 1997.
15. Godbeer 2002, 59.
16. Quoted in Lane 2000, 380.
17. Macfarlane 1979; Outhwaite 1982; Quaife 1979; Thompson 1989.
18. Quoted in Ryken 1986, 43.
19. Regnerus and Uecker 2011, 25.
20. Glenn and Marquardt 2001.
21. Regnerus and Uecker 2011, 34.
22. Regnerus 2007, 172.
23. Regnerus and Uecker 2011, 253, 258.
24. Prescott 1975, 11.
25. Bearman and Brückner 2001, 859.
26. Ibid., 861.
27. Rosenbaum 2009.
28. Michael et al. 1994, 116.
29. Laumann et al. 1994.
30. Friedman et al. 2009.

31. Waite and Joyner 2001.
32. Tavris and Sadd 1977.
33. Davidson, Darling, and Norton 1995.
34. Thompson 1983.
35. Singh, Walton, and Williams 1976.
36. Stark, Doyle, and Kent 1980; Stark et al. 1983; Stark and Bainbridge 1996.

CHAPTER 5
1. Freud 1927, 88.
2. Ellis 1988.
3. Ellis 1980, 637.
4. Allport 1960.
5. Ibid., 122.
6. Ostow 1990, 113
7. Carroll 1987, 491.
8. Levin 2001, viii.
9. Stark 1971.
10. Koenig, McCullough, and Larson 2001.
11. Virtue Ethics.
12. Stark and Maier 2008.
13. All cited in ibid.
14. Stark 1971.
15. Leak and Randall 1995.
16. Ray 1985; Watson et al. 2003.
17. Altemeyer 1981; 1988.
18. Altemeyer 1981, 219–20.
19. Koenig, McCullough, and Larson 2001, 127.
20. Spendlove et al. 1984.
21. Koenig, George, and Peterson 1998.
22. Koenig, McCullough, and Larson 2001, 124–28.
23. Moses et al. 1971.
24. Selznick and Steinberg 1969.
25. Koenig, McCullough, and Larson 2001.
26. Stark and Bainbridge 1996, 140.
27. Ray 1863 191.

28. Koenig, McCullough, and Larson 2001, 154–65.
29. For an extensive discussion, see Stark and Bainbridge 1996.
30. See Stark, *Sociology* (all editions).
31. Morselli 1879, 119.
32. Masaryk [1881] 1970, 85.
33. See Stark and Bainbridge 1996, chapter 3.
34. Data from the World Health Organization 2005.
35. Bainbridge and Stark 1981; Stack 1981; 1982; Stark and Bainbridge 1996; Stark, Doyle, and Rushing 1983.
36. Stark and Bainbridge 1996, chapter 3.
37. Ibid.
38. Burn 1953.
39. Stark 1998; 2011.
40. Hummer et al. 1999.
41. Medalie et al. 1973.
42. Oxman et al. 1995.
43. Koenig, McCullough, and Larson 2001, 250–63.
44. Colantonio, Kasl, and Ostfield 1992.
45. Koenig, McCullough, and Larson 2001, 270.
46. Levin and Vanderpool 1989, 74.
47. Dawkins 2006, 61.
48. Byrd 1988.
49. Sicher et al. 1998.
50. Aviles, Whelan, and Herneke 2001.
51. Hodge 2007.
52. Quoted in Carey 2004.
53. Krause 2011.

CHAPTER 6
1. Speech in New York, November 11, 1902.
2. Sablosky 2010, 3.

3. Phillips 2007, chapter 4.
4. Havens and Schervish 2007.
5. Brooks 2006, 202.
6. Borgonovi 2008; Regnerus, Smith, and Sikkink 1998.
7. Ruiter and de Graaf 2006.
8. Arts and Religion Survey 1999, available online from the American Religion Data Archive (ARDA).
9. Quoted in Schlesinger 1944 20.
10. Especially *Main Street* (1920) and *Babbitt* (1922).
11. Bellah et al. 1985, 50.
12. Ibid., 294.
13. Ibid., 155.
14. Baylor National Religion Survey 2007.
15. A fifteenth was dropped as uninterpretable.
16. Portions of this section have previously appeared in Stark 2008, chapter 18.
17. Based on the Baylor National Religion Surveys 2005; 2007; and the National Election Study 2004. That Evangelicals are not more active in politics than are others, see Stark 2008, chapter 18.
18. Tobin and Weinberg 2007.
19. Phillips 2007.
20. Harris 2006.
21. Rudin 2006.
22. Quoted in Hamburger 2002.
23. Barton 1993.
24. Blanshard 1958, 346.

CHAPTER 7
1. Weber, [1904–5] 1958.
2. Stark 2004.
3. Gilchrist 1969; Stark 2005.
4. McClellan and Reese 1988, 6–10.
5. Jeynes 2003; McKune and

Hoffman 2009; Muller and Ellison 2001; Regnerus 2003c; Regnerus and Elder 2003.
6. Regnerus, Smith, and Fritsch 2003.
7. Regnerus 2000; Regnerus and Elder 2003.
8. Jeynes 2003; 2007; Sikkink and Hernández 2003.
9. McKune and Hoffman 2009; Muller and Ellison 2001; Parcel and Dufer 2001.
10. McKune and Hoffman 2009.
11. Smith 2003, 19–20.
12. McKune and Hoffman 2009; Muller and Ellison 2001.
13. Coleman, Hoffer and Kilgore 1982; Jeynes 2003.
14. Bryk, Lee, and Holland 1993; Jeynes 2007.
15. Jeynes 2007.
16. Kalogrides 2009.
17. Reardon and Galindo 2009.
18. Department of Human and Health Services 2011.
19. Jeynes 2007.
20. Darnell and Sherkat 1997; Sherkat and Darnell 1999.
21. Beyerlein 2004.
22. Loury 2004.
23. Stark 2003.
24. Reiss 1961.

CHAPTER 8
1. Noll 1994, 3.
2. Hofstadter brought no similar charge of anti-intellectualism against the Communist Party, to which he belonged for several years. Although he left the party when Stalin signed his notorious pact with Hitler, Hofstadter remained a lifelong angry leftist, reaffirming, "I hate capitalism and everything

that goes with it" (in Foner
1992, 597).

3. Wuthnow 2003.
4. Hofstadter 1963, 48–49.
5. Ibid., 4.
6. Portions of this section are based on Stark 2008.
7. Bainbridge and Stark 1980.
8. Fox 1992; Goode 2000; Rice 2003.
9. For an entertaining tour of the entire spectrum of credulity, see Bader, Mencken, and Baker 2011.

10. Troeltsch [1912] 1931, 743, 794.
11. Drury 2004, 12.
12. Goldman 2012.
13. These statistics are based on small numbers of cases: nineteen Unitarians, fourteen Buddhists, and forty-one Jews.

CONCLUSION
1. Miller, Cohen, and Wiersma 1996.
2. Anderson 1999.

Bibliography

Adamczyk, Amy. 2009. "Socialization and Selection in the Link between Friend's Religiosity and the Transition to Sexual Intercourse." *Sociology of Religion* 70: 5–27.

Adorno, Theodor W., Else Frenkel-Brunswik, Daniel Levinson, and Nevitt Sanford. 1950. *The Authoritarian Personality*. New York: Harper and Row.

Ahlstrom, Sydney E. 1967. *Theology in America: The Major Protestant Voices from Puritanism to Neo-Orthodoxy*. Indianapolis: Bobbs-Merrill.

———. 1972. *A Religious History of the American People*. New Haven: Yale University Press.

Albrecht, Stan L., Bruce A. Chadwick, and David S. Alcorn. 1977. "Religiosity and Deviance." *Journal for the Scientific Study of Religion* 16: 2663–74.

Allan, Nicole. 2010. "Mike Huckabee, Comeback Kid?" *The Atlantic.com*, June 12.

Allport, Gordon W. 1960. *The Individual and His Religion*. New York: Macmillan.

Altemeyer, Bob. 1981. *Right-Wing Authoritarianism*. Winnipeg: University of Manitoba Press.

———. 1988. *Enemies of Freedom: Understanding Right-Wing Authoritarianism*. San Francisco: Jossey-Bass.

Alvarez, Lizette. 2003. "Tarbaek Journal: Fury, God, and the Pastor's Disbelief." *New York Times*, World Section, July 8.

Ananat, Elizabeth O., and Guy Michaels. 2008. "The Effect of Marital Breakup on the Income and Poverty of Women and Children." *Journal of Human Resources* 43: 611–29.

Anderson, David A. 1999. "The Aggregate Burden of Crime." *Journal of Law and Economics* 42: 611–42.

Asberg, Christer. 1990. "The Swedish Bible Commission and Project NT 81." In *Bible Reading in Sweden*, ed. Gunnar Hanson, 15–22. Uppsala: University of Uppsala.

Aviles, J. M., S. E. Whelan, and D. A. Herneke. 2001. "Intercessory Prayer and Cardiovascular Disease Progression in a Coronary Care Unit Population: A Randomized Controlled Trial." *Mayo Clinic Proceedings* 76: 1192–98.

Bader, Christopher F., Carson Mencken, and Joseph Baker. 2011. *Paranormal America: Ghost Encounters, UFO Sightings, Bigfoot Hunts, and Other Curiosities in Religion and Culture*. New York: New York University Press.

Bainbridge, W. S., and Rodney Stark. 1980. "Superstitions: Old and New." *Skeptical Inquirer* 4: 18–31.

———. 1981a. "Suicide, Homicide, and Religion: Durkheim Reassessed." *Annual Review of the Social Sciences of Religion* 5: 33–56.

———. 1981b. "Friendship, Religion and the Occult." *Review of Religious Research* 22: 313–27.

Bangs, Carl. 1972. "Deceptive Statistics." *Christian Century* 89: 852–53.

Bartkowski, John P., and W. Bradford Wilcox. 2000. "Conservative Protestant Child Discipline: The Case of Parental Yelling." *Social Forces* 7: 265–90.

Bartkowski, John P., and Xiaohe Xu. 2000. "Distant Patriarchs or Expressive Dads?" *Sociological Quarterly* 41: 465–85.

Barton, David. 1993. *The Myth of Separation*. Aledo, TX: Wallbuilder Press.

Bearman, Peter S., and Hannah Brückner. 2001. "Promising the Future: Virginity Pledges and First Intercourse." *American Journal of Sociology* 106: 859–12.

Beckford, James A. 1985. *Cult Controversies: The Societal Response to New Religions*. London: Tavistock Publications.

Bellah, Robert N., Richard Madsen, William Sullivan, Ann Swidler, and Steven M. Tipton. 1985. *Habits of the Heart: Individualism and Commitment in American Life*. Berkeley: University of California Press.

Berger, Peter L. 1969. *The Sacred Canopy*. New York: Doubleday Anchor Books.

———, Grace Davie, and Effie Fokas. 2008. *Religious America, Secular Europe?* Burlington, VT: Ashgate.

Beyerlein, Kraig. 2004. "Specifying the Impact of Conservative Protestantism on Educational Attainment." *Journal for the Scientific Study of Religion* 43: 505–18.

Bibby, Reginald W., and Merlin B. Brinkerhoff. 1973. "The Circulation of the Saints." *Journal for the Scientific Study of Religion* 12: 273–83.

———, 1983. "Circulation of the Saints Revisited." *Journal for the Scientific Study of Religion* 22:253–62.

Blanchard, Paul. [1949] 1958. *American Freedom and Catholic Power*. Boston: Beacon Press.

Bloodgood, James M., William Turnley, and Peter Mudrack. 2008. "The Influence of Ethics Instruction, Religiosity, and Intelligence on Cheating Behavior." *Journal of Business Ethics* 82: 557–71.

Borgonovi, Francesca. 2008. "Divided We Stand, United We Fall: Religious Pluralism, Giving, and Volunteering." *American Sociological Review* 73:105–28.

Brennan, Kathleen M., and Andrew S. London. 2001. "Are Religious People Nice People? Religiosity, Race, Interview Dynamics, and Perceived Cooperativeness." *Sociological Inquiry* 71: 129–44.

Brooks, Arthur C. 2006. *Who Really Cares?* New York: Basic Books.

Bryk, Anthony, Valerie Lee, and Peter Holland. 1993. *Catholic Schools and the Common Good*. Cambridge, MA: Harvard University Press.

Burdick, John. 1993. *Looking for God in Brazil*. Berkeley: University of California Press.

Burkett, Steven R., and Mervin White. 1974. "Hellfire and Delinquency: Another Look." *Journal for the Scientific Study of Religion* 13: 455–462.

Burn, A. R. 1953. "Hic breve vivitur: A Study of Expectations of Life in the Roman Empire." *Past and Present* 4: 2–31.

Byrd, Randolph C. 1988. "Positive Therapeutic Effects of Intercessory Prayer in a Coronary Care Unit Population." *Southern Medical Journal* 81: 826–29.

Call, Vaughn R., and Tim B. Heaton. 1997. "Religious Influence on Marital Stability." *Journal for the Scientific Study of Religion* 36: 382–92.

Capps, Donald. 1992. "Religion and Child Abuse: Perfect Together." *Journal for the Scientific Study of Religion* 32: 1–14.

———. 1995. *The Child's Song: The Religious Abuse of Children*. Louisville, KY: Westminster John Knox Press.

Carey, Benedict. 2004. "Can Prayers Heal? Critics Say Studies Go Past Science's Reach." *New York Times*, October 10.

Carroll, Michael P. 1987. "Praying the Rosary: The Anal-Erotic Origins of a Popular Catholic Devotion." *Journal for the Scientific Study of Religion* 26: 486–98.

Charles, Enid. 1936. *The Menace of Underpopulation*. London: Watts and Company.

Colantonio, A., S. V. Kasl, and A. M. Ostfeld. 1992. "Depressive Symptoms and Other Psychosocial Factors as Predictors of Stroke in the Elderly." *American Journal of Epidemiology* 136: 884–94.

Coleman, James S., Thomas Hoffer, and Sally Kilgore. 1982. *High School Achievement*. New York: Basic Books.

Cullen, Francis T. 2010. "Toward a Criminology of Religion: Comments on Johnson and Jang," *Contemporary Issues in Criminological Theory and Research: The Role of Social Institutions*, Richard Rosenfeld, Kenna Quinet, and Crystal Garcia (Eds.), 151–61.

Danzger, M. Herbert. 1989. *Returning to Tradition: The Contemporary Revival of Orthodox Judaism*. New Haven, CT: Yale University Press.

Darnell, Alfred, and Darren E. Sherkat. 1997. "The Impact of Protestant Fundamentalism on Educational Attainment." *American Sociological Review* 62: 306–15.

Davidman, Lynn. 1991. *Tradition in a Rootless World: Women Turn to Orthodox Judaism*. Berkeley: University of California Press.

Davidson, J. Kenneth, Carol Anderson Darling, and Laura Norton. 1995. "Religiosity and the Sexuality of Women: Sexual Behavior and Sexual Satisfaction Revisited." *Journal of Sex Research* 32: 235–43.

Dawkins, Richard. 2006. *The God Delusion*. Boston: Houghton Mifflin.

D'Emilio, John, and Estelle B. Freedman. 1997. *Intimate Matters: A History of Sexuality in America*. 2nd edition. Chicago: University of Chicago Press.

Department of Health and Human Services. 2011. *Head Start Impact Study*.

Dorrien, Gary. 2001. *The Making of American Liberal Theology: Imagining Progressive Religion, 1805–1900*. Louisville, KY: Westminster John Knox Press.

Drury, Nevill. 2004. *The New Age: Searching for the Spiritual Self.* London: Thames and Hudson.

Ebaugh, Helen Rose. 1993. *Women in the Vanishing Cloister: Organizational Decline of Catholic Religious Orders.* New Brunswick, NJ: Rutgers University Press.

Edwards, Paul. 1965. "Professor Tillich's Confusions." *Mind* 74: 192–214.

Egerton, John. 1974. *The Americanization of Dixie: The Southernization of America.* New York: Harper and Row.

Ellis, Albert. 1980. "Psychotherapy and Atheistic Values." *Journal of Consulting and Clinical Psychology* 48: 635–39.

———. 1988. "Is Religiosity Pathological?" *Free Inquiry* 18: 27–32.

Ellison, Christopher G. 1992. "Are Religious People Nice People? Evidence from the National Survey of Black Americans." *Social Forces* 71: 411–30.

———. 1996. "Conservative Protestantism and the Corporal Punishment of Children: Clarifying the Issues." *Journal for the Scientific Study of Religion* 35: 1–16.

———, and Kristin L. Anderson. 2001. "Religious Involvement and Domestic Violence among U.S. Couples." *Journal for the Scientific Study of Religion* 40: 269–86.

Evans, T. David, Francis T. Cullen, R. Gregory Dunaway, and Velmer S. Burton. 1995. "Religion and Crime Reexamined: The Impact of Religion, Secular Controls, and Social Ecology on Adult Criminality." *Criminology* 33: 195–224.

Finke, Roger, and Rodney Stark. 1992. *The Churching of America, 1776–1990: Winners and Losers in Our Religious Economy.* New Brunswick, NJ: Rutgers University Press.

Foner, Eric. 1992. "The Education of Richard Hofstadter." *The Nation* 254 (May 4): 597.

Foster, Thomas A. 1999. "Deficient Husbands: Manhood, Sexual Incapacity, and Male Marital Sexuality in Seventeenth-Century New England." *William and Mary Quarterly* 56: 723–74.

Fox, John W. 1992. "The Structure, Stability, and Social Antecedents of Reported Paranormal Experiences. " *Sociological Analysis* 53: 417–31.

Frejka, Tomas, and Charles F. Westoff. 2008. "Religion, Religiousness and Fertility in the US and in Europe." *European Journal of Population* 24: 5–31.

Freud, Sigmund. [1927] 1961. *Future of an Illusion.* Garden City, NY: Doubleday.

Friedman, Michelle, Ellen Labinsky, Talli Y. Rosenbaum, James Schmeidler, and Rachel Yehuda. 2009. "Observant Married Jewish Women and Sexual Life: An Empirical Study. *Conversations* 5 (Autumn): 37–59.

Gardner, J. W., and J. L. Lyon. 1977. "Low Incidence of Cervical Cancer in Utah." *Gynecologic Oncology* 5: 68–80.

Gaustad, Edwin S. 1987. *Faith of Our Fathers: Religion and the New Nation.* San Francisco: Harper and Row.

Gilchrist, John. 1969. *The Church and Economic Activity in the Middle Ages.* New York: St. Martin's Press.

Glenn, Norval, and Elizabeth Marquardt. 2001. *Hooking Up, Hanging Out, and Hoping for Mr. Right: College Women on Mating and Dating Today*. New York: Institute for American Values.

Godbeer, Richard. 2002. *Sexual Revolution in Early America*. Baltimore: Johns Hopkins University Press.

Goldman, David P. 2011. *How Civilizations Die (and Why Islam Is Dying Too)*. Washington, DC: Regnery.

Goldman, Marion. 2012. *The American Soul Rush: Esalen and the Rise of Spiritual Privilege*. New York: New York University Press.

Goode, Erich. 2000. *Paranormal Beliefs*. Prospect Heights, IL: Waveland Press.

Gordon, Antony, and Richard Horowitz. 1996. "Will Your Grandchildren Be Jews?" *Jewish Spectator* (Fall): 36–38.

Grasmick, Harold G., Karyl Kinsey, and John Cochran. 1991. "Denomination, Religiosity and Compliance with the Law." *Journal for the Scientific Study of Religion* 30: 99–107.

Greven, Philip. 1991. *Spare the Child: The Religious Roots of Punishment and the Psychological Impact of Physical Abuse*. New York: Alfred A. Knopf.

Grim, Brian J., and Roger Finke. 2006. "International Religion Indexes." *Interdisciplinary Journal for Research on Religion* 2 (1): 1–40.

Hadden, Jeffrey K. 1969. *The Gathering Storm in the Churches*. Garden City, NY: Doubleday.

Hamburger, Philip. 2002. *Separation of Church and State*. Cambridge: Harvard University Press.

Hammond, Guy B. 1964. "Tillich on the Personal God." *Journal of Religion* 44: 289–93.

Handlin, Oscar, ed. 1949. *This Was America*. Cambridge, MA: Harvard University Press.

Harris, Sam. 2006. *Letter to a Christian Nation*. New York: Random House.

Haught, James A. 1997. "Sex and God: Is Religion Twisted?" *Free Inquiry* 17 (Fall): 24–26.

Havens, John J., and Paul G. Schervish. 2007. *Geography and Giving*. Boston: Center on Wealth and Philanthropy.

Heilman, Samuel C. 2006. *Sliding to the Right: The Contest for the Future of American Jewish Orthodoxy*. Berkeley: University of California Press.

Higgins, P. C., and G. L. Albrecht. 1977. "Hellfire and Delinquency Revisited." *Social Forces* 55: 952–58.

Hindelang, Michael, Travis Hirschi, and Joseph Weis. 1981. *Measuring Delinquency*. Beverly Hills, CA: Sage.

Hirschi, Travis. 1969. *Causes of Delinquency*. Berkeley: University of California Press.

———, and Rodney Stark. 1969. "Hellfire and Delinquency." *Social Problems* 17: 202–13.

Hirschman, Charles, and Marilyn Butler. 1981. "Trends and Differentials in Breast Feeding: An Update." *Demography* 18: 39–54.

Hocking, William. 1912. *The Meaning of God in Human Experience*. New Haven, CT: Yale University Press.

Hodge, David R. 2007. "A Systematic Review of the Empirical Literature on Intercessory Prayer." *Research on Social Work Practice*. 17: 174–87.

Hofstadter, Richard. 1963. *Anti-Intellectualism in American Life*. New York: Knopf.

Hoge, Dean, and David Roozen, eds. 1979. *Understanding Church Growth and Decline*. New York: Pilgrim Press.

Hout, Michael, and Claude Fischer. 2002. "Americans with 'No Religion': Why Their Numbers Are Growing." *American Sociological Review* 67: 165–90.

Hummer, Robert A., Richard G. Rogers, Charles B. Nam, and Christopher G. Ellison. 1999. "Religious Involvement and U.S. Adult Mortality." *Demography* 36: 273–85.

Jeynes, William. 2003. *Religion, Education, and Academic Success*. Greenwich, CT: Information Age Publishing.

———. 2007. "Religion, Intact Families, and the Achievement Gap." *Interdisciplinary Journal of Research on Religion* 3: article 3.

Johnson, Byron. 2011. *More God, Less Crime*. West Conshohocken, PA: Templeton Press.

———, and Sung Joon Jang. 2012. "Crime and Religion: Assessing the Role of the Faith Factor." In *Contemporary Issues in Criminological Theory and Research: The Role of Social Institutions*, Richard Rosenfeld, Kenna Quinet, and Crystal Garcia, ed. , 117–49. Belmont, CA: Wadsworth.

Johnson, Martin A. 1973. "Family Life and Religious Commitment." *Review of Religious Research* 14: 144–50.

Kalogrides, Demetra. 2009. "Generational Status and Academic Achievement among Latino High School Students." *Sociological Perspectives* 52: 159–83.

Kaufmann, Eric. 2010. *Shall the Religious Inherit the Earth?* London: Profile Books.

Kelley, Dean. 1972. *Why Conservative Churches Are Growing*. New York: Harper and Row.

Kerley, Kent R., Todd Matthews, and Troy C. Blanchard. 2005. "Religiosity, Religious Participation, and Negative Prison Behaviors." *Journal for the Scientific Study of Religion* 44: 443–57.

King, Valarie. 2003. "The Influence of Religion on Fathers' Relationships with Their Children." *Journal of Marriage and Family* 65: 382–95.

Kluegel, James R. 1980. "Denominational Mobility." *Journal for the Scientific Study of Religion* 19: 26–39.

Koenig, H. G., L. K. George, and B.L. Peterson. 1998. "Religiosity and Remission from Depression in Medically Ill Older Patients." *America Journal of Psychiatry* 155: 536–42.

Koenig, Harold G., Michael E. McCullough, and David B. Larson. 2001. *Handbook of Religion and Health*. Oxford: Oxford University Press.

Krause, Neal. 2011. "The Perceived Prayers of Others, Stress, and Change in Depressive Symptoms over Time." *Review of Religious Research* 53: 341–56.

Landis, Judson T. 1960. "Religiousness, Family Relationships, and Family Values in Protestant, Catholic, and Jewish Families." *Marriage and Family Living* 22: 341–47.

Lane, Beldon C. 2000. "Two Schools of Desire: Nature and Marriage in Seventeenth-Century Puritanism." *Church History* 69: 372–402.

Laumann, Edward O., John H. Gagnon, Robert T. Michael, and Stuart Michaels. 1994. *The Social Organization of Sexuality.* Chicago: University of Chicago Press.

Lawrence, Raymond. 1985. "The Church and the Sexual Revolution." *Quarterly Review* 5: 32–45.

Leak, Gary K., and Brandy A. Randall. 1995. "Clarification of the Link between Right-Wing Authoritarianism and Religiousness: The Role of Maturity." *Journal for the Scientific Study of Religion* 34: 245–52.

Levin, Jeff. 2001. "Foreword." In Harold G. Koenig, Michael E. McCullough, and David B. Larson, *Handbook of Religion and Health*, vii–viii. Oxford: Oxford University Press.

———. 2010. "Religion and Mental Health: Theory and Research." *International Journal of Applied Psychoanalytic Studies*, www.interscience.wiley.com.

———, and Harold Y. Vanderpool. 1989. "Is Religion Therapeutically Significant for Hypertension?" *Social Science and Medicine* 29: 69–78.

Lichter, S. Robert, Stanley Rothman, and Linda Lichter. 1986. *The Media Elite.* Bethesda, MD: Adler and Adler.

Lodberg, Peter. 1989. "The Churches in Denmark." In *Danish Christian Handbook*, ed. Peter Briierly, 6–9. London: MARC Europe.

Loury, Linda D. 2004. "Does Church Attendance Really Increase Schooling?" *Journal for the Scientific Study of Religion* 43: 119–27.

Macfarlane, Alan. 1979. "Review Essay." *History and Theory* 18: 103–26.

Marshall, Paul, Lela Gilbert, and Roberta Green Ahmanson, eds. *Blind Spot: When Journalists Don't Get Religion.* Oxford: Oxford University Press.

Marty, Martin E. 1976. *A Nation of Behavers.* Chicago: University of Chicago Press.

Masaryk, Thomas G. [1881] 1970. *Suicide and the Meaning of Civilization.* Chicago: University of Chicago Press.

McAfee, Ward. 2008. "Religion and the Earth Crisis: An Indigenous American Perspective." *Population Press*, Summer.

McClellan, E. B., and W. J. Reese. 1988. *The Social History of American Education.* Urbana: University of Illinois Press.

McKune, Benjamin, and John P. Hoffman. 2009. "Religion and Academic Achievement among Adolescents." *Interdisciplinary Journal of Research on Religion* 5, article 10, www.religjournal.com.

Medalie, J. H., H. A. Kahn, H. N. Neufeld, E. Riss, U. Goldbourt, T. Perlstein, and D. Orin. 1973. "Myocardial Infarction over a Five-Year Period." *Journal of Chronic Disease* 26: 63–84.

Michael, Robert T., John H. Gagnon, Edward O. Laumann, and Gina Kolata. 1994. *Sex in America: A Definitive Survey.* Boston: Little, Brown.

Miller, Paul M. 1978. "Yes, Dean Kelly [sic], There Has Been Growth." *Gospel Herald*. March 28.

Miller, Perry. 1939. *The New England Mind in the Seventeenth Century*. Boston: Beacon Press.

Miller, Ted R., Mark A. Cohen, and Brian Wiersema. 1996. *Victim Costs and Consequences: A New Look*. Washington, DC: U.S. Department of Justice.

Morgan, Edmund S. 1942. "The Puritans and Sex." *New England Quarterly* 15: 591–607.

Morgan, S. Philip. 1983. "A Research Note on Religion and Morality: Are Religious People Nice People?" *Social Forces* 61: 683–92.

Morselli, Henry. 1879. *Suicide: An Essay on Comparative Moral Statistics*. New York: Appleton.

Moses, Lincoln, Allan Goldfarb, Charles Y. Glock, Rodney Stark, and Morris L. Eaton. 1971. "A Validity Study using the Leighton Instrument." *American Journal of Public Health* 61: 1785–93.

Muller, Chandra, and Christopher G. Ellison. 2001. "Religious Involvement, Social Capital, and Adolescents' Academic Progress." *Sociological Focus* 34: 155–83.

Myers, Norman. 2004a. "Europe's Population Decline: Problem or Opportunity?" *Population Press*, Winter.

———. 2004b. "Why Has Population Fallen Off Our Radar Screen?" *Population Press*, Fall.

Naguib, S. M., F. E. Lundin, and H. J. Davis. 1966. "Relation of Various Epidemiologic Factors to Cervical Cancer as Determinants of a Screening Program." *Obstetrics and Gynecology* 28: 451–59.

Neitz, Mary Jo. 1987. *Charisma and Community*. New Brunswick, NJ: Transaction.

Noll, Mark A. 1994. *The Scandal of the Evangelical Mind*. Grand Rapids: Eerdmans.

Ostow, Mortimer. 1990. "The Fundamentalist Phenomenon: A Psychological Perspective." In *The Fundamentalist Phenomenon: A View from Within, a Response from Without*, ed. Norman J. Cohen, 99–125. Grand Rapids: Eerdmans.

Outhwaite, R. B., ed. 1982. *Marriage and Society*. London: Palgrave Macmillan.

Oxman, T.E., D.H. Freeman, and E.D. Manheimer. 1995. "Lack of Social Participation or Religious Strength and Comfort as Risk Factors for Death After Cardiac Surgery in the Elderly." *Psychosomatic Medicine* 57:5-15.

Parcel, Toby L., and Mikaela J. Dufur. 2001. "Capital at Home and at School: Effects on Student Achievement." *Social Forces* 79: 881–911.

Pearce, Lisa D., and William G. Axinn. 1998. "The Impact of Family Religious Life on the Quality of Mother-Child Relations." *American Sociological Review* 63: 810–28.

Perrin, Robin D. 2000. "Religiosity and Honesty: Continuing the Search for the Consequential Dimension." *Review of Religious Research* 41: 534–44.

———, Paul Kennedy, and Donald E. Miller. 1997. "Examining the Sources of Conservative Church Growth." *Journal for the Scientific Study of Religion* 36: 71–80.

Perry, Everett L. 1973. "Review." *Review of Religious Research* 14: 198–200.

Pettersson, Thorlief. 1990. "The Holy Bible in Secularized Sweden." In *Bible Reading in Sweden*, ed. Gunnar Hanson, 23–45. Uppsala: University of Uppsala.

Phillips, Kevin. 2007. *American Theocracy*. New York: Viking.

Piliavin, Jane Allyn, and Hong-Wen Charng. 1990. "Altruism: A Review of Recent Theory and Research." *Annual Review of Sociology* 16:27065.

Powell, Milton B, ed. 1967. *The Voluntary Church*. New York: Macmillan.

Prescott, James W. 1975. "Body Pleasure and the Origins of Violence." *Bulletin of the Atomic Scientists* (November): 10–20.

Putnam, Robert D. 2000. *Bowling Alone*. New York: Simon and Schuster.

Quaife, G. R. 1979. *Wanton Wenches and Wayward Wives*. New Brunswick, NJ: Rutgers University Press.

Ray, Isaac. 1863. *Mental Hygiene*. Boston: Ticknor and Fields.

Ray, John J. 1985. "Defective Validity in the Altemeyer Authoritarianism Scale." *Journal of Social Psychology* 125: 271–72.

Reardon, Sean F., and Claudia Galindo. 2009. "The Hispanic-White Achievement Gap in Math and Reading in the Elementary Grades." *American Educational Research Journal* 46: 853–91.

Reeves, Thomas C. 1996. *The Empty Church*. New York: The Free Press.

Regnerus, Mark. 2000. "Shaping Schooling Success: Religious Socialization and Educational Outcomes in Metropolitan Public Schools." *Journal for the Scientific Study of Religion* 39: 363–70.

———. 2003a. "Moral Communities and Adolescent Delinquency: Religious Contexts and Community Social Control." *Sociological Quarterly* 44: 523–54.

———. 2003b. "Linking Lives, Faith, and Behavior: Intergenerational Religious Influence on Adolescent Delinquency." *Journal for the Scientific Study of Religion* 42: 189–203.

———. 2003c. "Religion and Positive Adolescent Outcomes: A Review of Research and Theory." *Review of Religious Research* 44: 394–413.

———. 2007. *Forbidden Fruit: Sex and Religion in the Lives of American Teenagers*. New York: Oxford University Press.

———, and Glen H. Elder Jr. 2003. "Staying on Track in School: Religious Influences in High- and Low-Risk Settings." *Journal for the Scientific Study of Religion* 42: 633–49.

Regnerus, Mark, Christian Smith, and Melissa Fritsch. 2003. *Religion in the Lives of American Adolescents: A Review of the Literature*. A Research Report of the National Study of Youth and Religion. #3. Chapel Hill: University of North Carolina.

Regnerus, Mark, Christian Smith, and David Sikkink. 1998. " Who Gives to the Poor?" *Journal for the Scientific Study of Religion* 37: 481–93.

Regnerus, Mark, and Jeremy Uecker. 2011. *Premarital Sex in America*. New York: Oxford University Press.

Reiss, Albert J. 1991. *Occupations and Social Status*. New York: Free Press.

Rice, Tom W. 2003. "Believe It or Not: Religious and Other Paranormal Beliefs in the United States." *Journal for the Scientific Study of Religion* 42: 95–106.

Riesman, David, in collaboration with Nathan Glazer and Reuel Denny. 1950. *The Lonely Crowd: A Study of the Changing American Character*. New Haven, CT: Yale University Press.

Roof, Wade Clark, and William McKinney. 1987. *American Mainline Religion: Its Changing Shape and Future*. New Brunswick, NJ: Rutgers University Press.

Rosenbaum, Janet Elise. 2009. "Patient Teenagers? A Comparison of the Sexual Behavior of Virginity Pledgers and Matched Nonpledgers." *Pediatrics* 123: 110–20.

Rowe, William L. 1962. "The Meaning of 'God' in Tillich's Theology." *Journal of Religion* 42: 274–86.

Rudin, Rabbi James. 2006. *The Baptizing of America: The Religious Right's Plans for the Rest of Us*. New York: Thunder Mouth Press.

Rudner, Lawrence M. 1999. "Scholastic Achievement and Demographic Characteristics of Home School Students in 1998." *Education Policy Analysis Archives* 7: 1–33.

Ruiter, Stijn, and Nan Dirk de Graaf. 2006. "National Context, Religiosity and Volunteering: Results from 53 Countries." *American Sociological Review* 71: 191–210.

Russell, Bertrand. 1970. *Marriage and Morals*. New York: Liveright.

Rydenfelt, Sven. 1985. "Sweden and Its Bishops." *Wall Street Journal*, August 21, A25.

Ryken, Leland. 1986. *Worldly Saints: The Puritans as They Really Were*. Grand Rapids, MI: Zondervan.

Sablosky, Roy (writing as Yashwata). 2010. "The Myth of Christian Charity (part 1)." http://yashwata.info/2010/07/15/charity1/

Schlesinger, Arthur M. 1944. "Biography of a Nation of Joiners." *American Historical Review* 50: 1–25.

Schmied, Gerhard. 1996. "US-Televangelism on German TV." *Journal of Contemporary Religion* 11: 95–99.

Schwadel, Philip. 2011. "The Effects of Education on Americans' Religious Practices, Beliefs, and Affiliations." *Review of Religious Research* 53: 161–82.

Selthoffer, Steve. 1997. "German Government Harasses Charismatic Christians." *Charisma* (June): 22–24.

Selznick, Gertrude J., and Stephen Steinberg. 1969. *The Tenacity of Prejudice*. New York: Harper and Row.

Sherkat, Darren E., and Alfred Darnell. 1999. "The Effect of Parents' Fundamentalism on Children's Educational Attainment." *Journal for the Scientific Study of Religion* 38: 23–35.

Sherkat, Darren E., and John Wilson. 1995. "Preferences, Constraints, and Choices in Religious Markets: An Examination of Religious Switching and Apostasy." *Social Forces* 73: 993–1026.

Shibley, Mark. 1991. "The Southernization of American Religion: Testing a Hypothesis." *Sociological Analysis* 52: 159–74.

Sicher, F., E. Targ, D. Moore, and H. S. Smith. 1998. "A Randomized Double-Blind Study of the Effect of Distant Healing in a Population with Advanced AIDS: Report of a Small Study." *Western Journal of Medicine* 169: 356–63.

Sikkink, David, and Edwin I. Hernández. 2003. *Religion Matters: Predicting Schooling Success among Latino Youth*. Notre Dame, IN: Institute for Latino Studies.

Singh, B. Krishna, Bonnie L. Walton, and J. Sherwood Williams. 1976. "Extramarital Sexual Permissiveness: Conditions and Contingencies." *Journal of Marriage and Family* 38: 701–12.

Smith, Adam. [1776] 1981. *An Inquiry into the Nature and Causes of the Wealth of Nations*. 2 vols. Indianapolis: Liberty Fund.

Smith, Chad Powers. 1954. *Yankees and God*. New York: Heritage House.

Smith, Christian. 1998. *American Evangelicalism*. Chicago: University of Chicago Press.

———. 2003. "Religious Participation and Parental Moral Expectations and Supervision of American Youth." *Review of Religious Research* 44: 414–24.

Smith, Daniel Scott. 1985. "The Dating of the American Sexual Revolution: Evidence and Interpretation." In *Reply to Myth: Perspectives on Intimacy*, ed. John F. Crosby. New York: John Wiley.

Spendlove, D.C., D.W. West, and W.M. Stanish. 1984. "Risk Factors and the Prevalence of Depression in Mormon Women." *Social Science and Medicine* 18:491-495.

Stack, Steven. 1981. "Suicide and Religion: A Comparative Analysis." *Sociological Focus* 14: 207–20.

———. 1982. "Suicide: A Decade Review of the Sociological Literature." *Deviant Behavior* 4: 41–66.

Stark, Rodney. 1971. "Psychopathology and Religious Commitment." *Review of Religious Research* 12: 165–76.

———. 1984. "Religion and Conformity: Reaffirming a *Sociology* of Religion." *Sociological Analysis* 46: 18–27.

———. 1988. *Sociology*. 3rd edition. Belmont, CA: Wadsworth.

———. 1992. *Sociology*. 4th edition. Belmont, CA: Wadsworth.

———. 1993. *North American Crime and Delinquency*. Seattle: MicroCase Corporation.

———. 1996. "Religion as Context: Hellfire and Delinquency One More Time." *Sociology of Religion* 57: 163–73.

———. 1998. "Live Longer, Healthier, and Better: The Untold Benefits of Becoming Christian in the Ancient World." *Christian History* 17: 28–30.

———. 2003. *For the Glory of God: How Monotheism Led to Reformations, Science, Witch-Hunts and the End of Slavery*. Princeton, NJ: Princeton University Press.

———. 2004. "Putting an End to Ancestor Worship." *Journal for the Scientific Study of Religion* 43: 465–75.

———. 2004. *The Victory of Reason: How Christianity Led to Freedom, Capitalism, and Western Success*. New York: Random House.

———. 2007. *Sociology*. 10th edition. Belmont, CA: Wadsworth.

———. 2008. *What Americans Really Believe*. Waco, TX: Baylor University Press.

———. 2011. *The Triumph of Christianity: How the Jesus Movement Became the World's Largest Religion*. San Francisco: HarperOne.

———, and William Sims Bainbridge. 1985. *The Future of Religion: Secularization, Revival and Cult Formation*, Berkeley: University of California Press.

———. 1996. *Religion, Deviance, and Social Control*. New York: Routledge.

Stark, Rodney, W. S. Bainbridge, Robert Crutchfield, Daniel P. Doyle, and Roger Finke. 1983. "Crime and Delinquency in the Roaring Twenties." *Journal of Research in Crime and Delinquency* 20: 4–23.

Stark, Rodney, Daniel P. Doyle, and Lori Kent. 1980. "Rediscovering Moral Communities: Church Membership and Crime." In *Understanding Crime*, ed. Travis Hirschi and Michael Gottfredson, 43–52. Beverly Hills, CA: Sage.

Stark, Rodney, Daniel P. Doyle, and Jesse Lynn Rushing. 1983. "Beyond Durkheim: Religion and Suicide." *Journal for the Scientific Study of Religion*, 22: 120–31.

Stark, Rodney, and Roger Finke, 2000. *Acts of Faith: Explaining the Human Side of Religion*. Berkeley: University of California Press.

Stark, Rodney, Bruce D. Foster, Charles Y. Glock, and Harold E.Quinley. 1971. *Wayward Shepherds: Prejudice and the Protestant Clergy*. New York: Harper and Row.

Stark, Rodney and Charles Y. Glock. 1968. *American Piety*. Berkeley: University of California Press.

Stark, Rodney, and Laurence R. Iannaccone. 1994. "A Supply-Side Reinterpretation of the 'Secularization' of Europe." *Journal for the Scientific Study of Religion* 33: 230–52.

Stark, Rodney, and Massimo Introvigne. 2003. *Dio é Tornato: Indagine Sulla Rivincita Delle Religioni in Occidente* (God Is Back: An Enquiry into the Revival of Religions in the West). Casale Monferrato: Piemme.

Stark, Rodney, Lori Kent, and Daniel P. Doyle. 1982. "Religion and Delinquency: The Ecology of a `Lost' Relationship." *Journal of Research in Crime and Delinquency* 19: 4–24.

Stark, Rodney, and Jared Maier. 2008. "Faith and Happiness." *Review of Religious Research* 50: 120–25.

Straus, Murray. 1994. *Beating the Devil Out of Them: Corporal Punishment in American Families and Its Effects on Children*. Boston: Lexington Books.

Sullivan, Amy. 2011. "Elitist Ridicule Fuels Palin's Faithful Base." *USA Today Forum* (online), http://www.usatoday.com/news/opinion/forum/2011-04-11-column11_ST_N.htm.

Tavris, Carol, and Susan Sadd. 1977. *The Redbook Report on Female Sexuality*. New York: Delacorte.

Thompson, Anthony P. 1983. "Extramarital Sex: A Review of the Research Literature." *Journal of Sex Research* 19: 1–22.

Thompson, Roger. 1989. *Sex in Middlesex: Popular Mores in a Massachusetts County, 1649–1699*. Amherst: University of Massachusetts Press.

Tillich, Paul. 1951. *Systematic Theology*. Volume 1. Chicago: University of Chicago Press.

———. 1952. *The Courage to Be*. New Haven: Yale University Press.

———. [1957] 2009. *Dynamics of Faith*. San Francisco: HarperOne.

Tittle, Charles R., and Michael R. Welch. 1983. "Religiosity and Deviance: Towards a Contingency Theory of Constraining Effects." *Social Forces* 61: 653–82.

Tobin, Gary A., and Aryeh K. Weinberg. 2007. *Profiles of the American University.* Vol. 2: *Religious Beliefs and Behavior of College Faculty.* San Francisco: Institute for Jewish and Community Research.

Troeltsch, Ernst. [1912] 1931. *The Social Teaching of the Christian Churches.* London: George Allen and Unwin.

Wainwright, William J. 1971. "Paul Tillich and Arguments for the Existence of God." *Journal of the American Academy of Religion* 39: 171–85.

Waite, Linda J., and Kara Joyner. 2001. "Emotional Satisfaction and Physical Pleasure in Sexual Unions: Time Horizon, Sexual Behavior, and Sexual Exclusivity." *Journal of Marriage and Family* 63: 247–64.

Wallace, John M., and Tyrone A. Forman. 1998. "Religion's Role in Promoting Health and Reducing Risk among American Youth." *Health Education and Behavior* 25: 721–41.

Watson, P. J., Pauline Sawyers, Ronald J. Morris, Mark L. Carpenter, Rachel S. Jimenez, Katherine A. Jonas, and David L. Robinson. 2003. "Reanalysis within a Christian Ideological Surround: Relationships of Intrinsic Religious Orientation with Fundamentalism and Right-Wing Authoritarianism." *Journal of Psychology and Theology* 31: 315–28.

Weber, Max. [1904–5] 1958. *The Protestant Ethic and the Spirit of Capitalism.* New York: Charles Scribner's Sons.

Welch, Michael R., Charles R. Tittle, and Harold G. Grasmick. 2006. "Christian Religiosity, Self-Control and Social Conformity." *Social Forces* 84: 1605–23.

Wertheimer, Jack. 1993. *A People Divided: Judaism in Contemporary America.* New York: Basic Books.

Whitefield, George. [1756] 1969. *George Whitefield's Journals.* Gainesville, FL: Scholar's Facsimiles and Reprints.

Whyte, William. 1957. *The Organization Man.* New York: Doubleday Anchor Books.

Wilcox, W. Bradford. 1998. "Conservative Protestant Child-Rearing: Authoritarian or Authoritative?" *American Sociological Review* 63: 796–809.

———. 2002. "Religion, Convention, and Paternal Involvement." *Journal of Marriage and Family* 64: 780–92.

———. 2004. *Soft Patriarchs, New Men.* Chicago: University of Chicago Press.

Wilson, Bryan. 1966. *Religion in Secular Society.* London: C. A. Watts.

Woodward, Kenneth L. 1993. "Dead End for the Mainline?" *Newsweek.* Aug. 9:47.

Wuthnow, Robert. 2003. *All in Sync: How Music and Art Are Revitalizing American Religion.* Berkeley: University of California Press.

Index

Blanshard, Paul, 131
Blavatsky, Helena, 159
blood donation, 54
"Body Pleasure and the Origins of
    Violence" (Prescott), 83
Bowling Alone (Putnam), 121
Bradburn, Norman, 95
Brückner, Hannah, 83
Buddhism, 114, 162
Burdick, John, 15
Bush, George W., 124, 157
Byrd, Randolph, 108–9

capitalism, 133
Capps, Donald, 71
Carroll, Michael P., 94
Catholic Church. See Roman
    Catholicism
Catholic schools, 137
Causes of Delinquency (Hirschi), 45
Celestine Prophecy, The (Redfield),
    160–61
Channing, William Ellery, 21
charitable donations, 117–18, 166
Charles, Enid, 59
chastity pledging, 82–85
Chesterton, G. K., 155
child birth rates. See fertility and
    population growth
child rearing. See also education
    delinquency and, 71–72
    discipline, 70–71
    education and homeschooling,
        72–76
    parent-child relationships, 68–70
    religious differences and, 68
    supervision, 70
Christianity. See specific topics, such
    as Evangelicals
church and state. See politics; sepa-
    ration of church and state
church attendance and member-
    ship. See also participation,
    religious
    charitable donations and, 118

credulity and, 158, 162
crime rates and, 49
divorce and, 67
economic hardship and, 144–46
education and, 140–41
fertility and, 62–63
generosity and, 116–17
mainline decline, 16–20, 25–26
market shares (1776–1850), 12–13
marriage happiness and, 66
music and arts and, 151–53
occupational prestige and, 142
organizational membership and,
    124
parent-child relationships and,
    68–69
physical health and, 106–7
Putnam on, 121
reading and, 149–51
regional patterns of, 46–47
sex practices and, 81–82
suicide rates and, 105
wealth and, 143–44
churches growth and decline, 16–20
Church of Denmark, 33–34
Church of Sweden, 34–35
church shopping, 14
citizenship. See prosocial behavior
    and citizenship
civic participation, 120–24
clergy, 10, 11–12
college, 75, 81, 139–41. See also edu-
    cation
Colonial America, 9–11, 78–80, 133
Colson, Chuck, 51
competition. See pluralism and
    competition, religious
conformity, critique of, 120–21
conservative churches, growth of,
    18–20
Conservative Jews. See Jews and
    Judaism
conservative Protestants. See also
    Evangelicals
    authoritarianism and, 97

Hasidic Jews. *See* Jews and Judaism
Hatt, Paul, 141
Hauerwas, Stanley, 26
Head Start Program, 138, 164–65
health, mental. *See* mental health
health, physical
  church attendance and, 106–7
  financial implications, 165–166
  prayer and faith healing, 108–10
  religious effects, efforts to explain,
    107–8
Heard, Mary, 78
high culture, 148–53
High School and Beyond Study,
  136–37
Hinduism, 114
Hirschi, Travis, 45
Hispanic Americans and education,
  72–73, 134, 137, 138
Hitler, Adolf, 96
Hocking, William Ernest, 21–22
Hoffer, Eric, 168
Hofstadter, Richard, 147, 148, 151, 152
home ownership, 143–44
homeschooling, 73–76, 164
Honest to God (Robinson), 33
honesty, 53
Hoover, Herbert, 115
Huckabee, Mike, 6

Index of Occult and Paranormal
  Belief, 157–58
individualism, 120–21
intellectual life
  claims of religion as incompatible
    with, 147, 148
  faith and credulity, 154–62
  music and arts, 151–53
  reading, 148–51
  religious intellectualism, 153–54
International Social Survey Project,
  61, 66–67
intrinsic religion, 93–94, 99–100
investment in stock market,
  143–44

Iowa Test of Basic Skills, 74
Islam, 114

jailhouse conversions, 50–51
Jerrad, Elizabeth, 79
Jerrad, Robert, 79
Jews and Judaism
  credulity and, 162
  fertility rates, 63–64
  generosity and, 114
  health and, 107
  Orthodox growth and Reform
    decline, 27
  sexuality of, 88
Jeynes, William, 139
joiners, 120–24

Kant, Immanuel, 104
Kaufmann, Eric, 63
Kelly, Dean M., 16–18
Kerry, John, 157
King, Valerie, 69

laws. *See also* crime; politics
  favoring established churches,
    31–32
  against homeschooling, 73–74
  Italian tax law, 29
  on separation of church and state,
    126–27
leftists, radical, 24–26
Levin, Jeff, 94, 107–8
Lewis, Sinclair, 120
liberal and mainline Protestantism.
  See also Europe
  credulity and, 162
  decline of, 16–20, 25–26
  European state churches modeled
    after, 33–35
  Evangelicals among, 126
  modernist theology in, 20–24
  permissive religion, poverty of,
    15–16
  radical leftists and socialism,
    24–26